# Principles of Advanced English
# Composition

## DANTES/DSST* Test Study Guide

All rights reserved. This Study Guide, Book and Flashcards are protected under the US Copyright Law. No part of this book or study guide or flashcards may be reproduced, distributed or stored in a retrieval system, or transmitted in any form or by any means, electronic, mechanical, photocopying, recording, or otherwise, without the prior written permission of the publisher Breely Crush Publishing, LLC.

## © 2026 Breely Crush Publishing, LLC

*DSST is a registered trademark of The Thomson Corporation and its affiliated companies, and does not endorse this book.*

*971010221143*

Copyright ©2003 - 2026, Breely Crush Publishing, LLC.

All rights reserved.

This Study Guide, Book and Flashcards are protected under the US Copyright Law. No part of this publication may be reproduced, distributed or stored in a retrieval system, or transmitted in any form or by any means, electronic, mechanical, photocopying, recording, or otherwise, without the prior written permission of the publisher Breely Crush Publishing, LLC.

Published by Breely Crush Publishing, LLC
10808 River Front Parkway
South Jordan, UT 84095
www.breelycrushpublishing.com

ISBN-10: 1-61433-683-0
ISBN-13: 978-1-61433-683-9

Printed and bound in the United States of America.

*DSST is a registered trademark of The Thomson Corporation and its affiliated companies, and does not endorse this book.*

# Table of Contents

I. Types of Writing ..................................................................................................2
II. Elements of Effective Writing ............................................................................4
    1. Pre-Writing Strategies/Content Generation ..................................................4
    2. Invention Techniques ....................................................................................5
    3. Reading, Thinking, Analyzing, and Discussion ............................................7
    4. Final Steps Before Writing ...........................................................................9
    5. Drafting .......................................................................................................10
    6. Editing ........................................................................................................11
III. Reading and Writing Arguments .....................................................................13
    1. Overview of an Argument ..........................................................................14
    2. Evidence .....................................................................................................16
    3. Putting It Together: How to Construct a Strong Argument .......................18
    4. Reading Arguments ....................................................................................19
    5. Judging the Strength of an Argument ........................................................20
    6. Rottenberg Method .....................................................................................22
IV. Sources: Where to Find Information, Evaluate, and Cite in Paper ..................22
    1. Secondary Sources Overview .....................................................................23
    2. Evaluating Secondary Sources ...................................................................23
    3. Using Sources .............................................................................................25
    4. Citing and Documenting ............................................................................26
V. Conclusion ........................................................................................................31
Sample Test Questions .........................................................................................32
Test-Taking Strategies .........................................................................................64
Test Preparation ...................................................................................................64
Legal Note ............................................................................................................65

With the advent of computers, the sharing of information has become quicker, easier, and more widely available. Fiber optic cables, wireless receivers and transmitters, and personal laptops have made the transportation of information almost instantaneous; indeed, in our day and age, information and the access to it has become so open that anyone can learn, find answers, and keep up-to-date on news as it is happening on the ground. In turn, as these answers become easier to acquire, the questions have grown larger and more abstract, leading to new forms of thought and inquiry totally different than the ones our forebears were wrangling with. And yet, while we continue to creatively confront these new questions, key themes remain important to the grand narrative, tying us intimately to our past.

The first continuing theme is that information's status as either free or able to be "owned" in some way continues to be at the forefront of debates. For centuries, holding key bits of information has been integral to the running of societies. Military intelligence, corporate secrets, governmental actions/plans, and even knowledge pertaining to spirituality have often been closely guarded through such means of confidentiality as codes and cryptograms. While it once was true that someone who knew something important could simply not talk, hide the document, or keep the document from public eyes in a secure location, the internet has leveled this ability. All it takes today is simply placing private files and information on a thumb drive, carrying it from the location, and emailing it to others. The information can be encrypted, each "bit" of information jumbled into chaos as it is sent across the internet, but once it gets released, it is there forever. One need only look at the Snowden affair to understand this.

The second is a theme that is far more benign in its appearance, but all the more important as you read this text and take the skills included in your own life: all of this information, be it guarded or open, or on the internet or in a book, is *written* in some sort of understandable language. Indeed, writing is a crucial instrument of the human condition, the way we communicate to others when not face-to-face. To illustrate the importance of such an action, historians—in their attempt to classify, categorize, and analyze history—commonly divide history into two large segments: prehistory and history. The literal split between the two is writing. Writing indicates the entrance of a human society into a period organized enough to impart knowledge and information onto a surface, which can then be analyzed textually by historians to understand the age.

As can be seen, writing is one of the most important actions human beings have undertaken throughout history. It continues to be an indelible part of the human experience, something we are taught to do at a young age and never stop doing throughout our lifetimes. As you approach your entrance to the professional world, learning to write and write effectively becomes ever more important. Recalling that language is a two-way street—it takes both talking and listening—writing that language is also comprised of dual, symbiotic strands: physically writing and reading that writing. Therefore, learning to write effectively will necessarily strengthen your ability to read and understand others. Both processes together will in turn help you to think critically, and in our age of "fake news" and "clickbait" this ability is central to knowing right from wrong and truth from untruth.

# I. Types of Writing

As such, writing can be divided into various categories that make it easier to comprehend and, in turn, write and read. These "formats" can be found both alone and in conjunction with each other, with many books including multiple forms of writing wrapped in one. Before jumping into the types of writing, it is best to understand that in writing and communicating a specific message, the audience has to be remembered. Certain forms of writing are best for certain audiences, while others can be used to communicate effectively across the board. Figuring out what you aim to communicate, who the audience is, and how to most effectively get your point across is crucial. In each of these categories, "target" audiences and how those can be coupled with the other forms will be covered, helping you decide which type of writing you would like to use.

## A. NARRATIVE WRITING

The first category of writing is the narrative. Though the narrative can be either fiction or nonfiction, it tends to follow a certain framework. It is a story, told in a particular sequence, that at times includes a narrator—which can be yourself—a particular setting or settings, and a conflict and resolution that are found by the end of the story. The narrative form of writing should be the most recognizable: we come into contact with it whenever we tell or read a story. As such, whether it is one of the countless fairy tales told to us in our youth, a fantasy book series we read as teens, or a featured article in a magazine, narratives can be ubiquitous.

You can use the narrative form in a number of different ways, but the most important thing to consider is the fact that the very framework of the narrative lends itself to being used both alone and in conjunction with the other categories of writing. For example, you may have noticed that many nonfictions books—particularly history and any social science books—utilize narratives to construct the book or to provide a useful anecdote to support the writing's argument. We will get to argumentative writing later, but for now suffice it to say that the narrative is one of the most flexible writing forms that can be used to effectively communicate whatever you want in writing.

## B. INFORMATIVE WRITING

The informative writing category is very similar, particularly in structure, to the narrative, yet it does have a few key differences that must be kept in mind. A piece of informative writing needs to do exactly that: *inform* or *educate* the reader on a specific topic. On the one hand, it is similar to the narrative in that it must have a clear beginning, middle, and end, though it does not need the other elements—particularly characters, conflicts, and resolutions. On the other hand, this form of writing tends to be articulated in an essay, which is why this form is most commonly known as the "informative essay" or "expository essay." As such, the essay is used primarily to inform the audience of a specific matter, and should maintain this focus.

## C. ARGUMENTATIVE WRITING

As the name suggests, argumentative writing aims to lay out a key argument and support it through the provision of pieces of evidence. This category is always nonfiction, and is found particularly through pieces of academic and legal writing. As such, learning how to articulate and understand a written argument is paramount to your current education as a critical thinker and your future success. We will get to how to build a successful argument, and recognize it in others' writings, later in this chapter.

## D. PERSUASIVE WRITING

Again, as the name suggests, a persuasive writing piece aims to *persuade* a reader to think in a certain manner or take a certain action. Persuasive writing can take many forms, from the longer memos that suggest an individual, notably a political leader, undertake certain actions to marketing campaigns that tempt you into buying a company's product. On the one hand, persuasive writing can often take the form of an argument—which mixes both persuasive and argumentative writing together—to convince you to do something while, on the other hand, persuasive writing oftentimes appeals to your emotions, preferences, or beliefs. As is hinted at above, a successful piece of persuasive writing can be used in conjunction with argumentative, informative, and narrative writing types.

## E. CRITICAL RESPONSE

As with the other types, the critical response type of writing is doing exactly what its name is telling you: it is responding to another individual's thoughts, writing, art, or actions. The author of a critical response piece takes a position either fully or partially in opposition to the argument of the other writer. Additionally, the critical response writer will oftentimes bring in outside research to support their side of the argument in order to weaken the other's argument. Critical responses are found particularly in newspaper op-eds, periodicals, academic journals, and in academic books.

#  II. Elements of Effective Writing

Now that we have covered the five basic types of writing, it is time to jump in and begin describing how you can start writing. The following section will cover the entirety of the writing process, from the initial idea, to the searching and discovery of evidence, to the organization of that evidence, and then finally to the writing. Following this will be a final subsection on the editing phase which, to many writers (myself included!), is the most important and crucial phase to writing.

A quick note is be in order before jumping into the section: it is the experience of this author that, while the following is indeed a rough overview of the process, rarely does writing go in this order. Oftentimes, initial ideas and content generation are stumbled upon when reading others' writing, with the evidence building up before you arrive at the argument. Don't worry if your writing style doesn't follow this pathway. Each of these is meant as an aid, and if it doesn't help you in terms of order, perhaps it can help if you are stuck in the middle of writing.

## *1. PRE-WRITING STRATEGIES/CONTENT GENERATION*

A wise professor once told me that the hardest part about writing is getting started. While he didn't necessarily mean that we have to actively seek out inspiration, which can be nauseatingly tiresome, what he did mean was the process of taking the ideas floating around in your head and putting them into some sort of form that can be researched. Indeed, this step is extraordinarily difficult and can often stall writers or force them to abandon the desire to write in the first place. A true tragedy, that.

Yet there are ways to prime your mind to find something to write on. These steps, though a tad complicated at the beginning, become so overwhelmingly easy with practice that your brain will adjust, causing you to follow these techniques without even trying. Indeed, this author has practiced these steps for so long that the problem becomes one of too many ideas to write on, which in turn shifts into a problem of deciding which ideas are crucial to write on now and which can be placed on the backburner. Much like your reading skills, these steps will become so easy as to almost become subconscious with time and practice.

The first pre-writing strategy that can help formulate content is to simply ask a question. Simple enough it seems at first, but then try to do it without practicing before. Maybe you begin to realize you don't know what question to ask. Or you may think your question is stupid. In regard to both of these, I would ask you to do me a favor, dear reader: bundle both of those up in your mind, and toss them in the wastebasket. No question is too stupid to ask, and if you don't know what question to ask, just start listing them. After your brain starts to stop feeding questions, go back and read through them a few times. As you will most likely see, many of the questions will be asking the same thing, and you can take that common question and begin running it down.

This next step is where things begin to get fun. Though you are not quite there yet, the question can begin leading you to places to find possible sources that can help you answer that question. We will get further into this research phase in the next sub-section, but suffice it to say for now that there are resources you can turn to in order to get an idea of where you can find information. The most obvious is the internet: you would be surprised what will come of simply googling your question. More often than not, someone else out there has the same question and has asked it, accumulating responses that can begin to point you in the right direction. If you don't see any of these, pay attention to what the results are pointing you toward and take a few moments to understand why the search engine responded to your question in this way: this can help you find additional avenues.

## *2. INVENTION TECHNIQUES*

While coming up with questions and narrowing them down is the best method for pre-writing ideas, at times questioning doesn't work. If the questions appear to be too varied or you can't seem to come up with any questions in general, there are other techniques you can take to find writing ideas. These methods can help you formulate ideas that can then be further developed, researched, and focused through extra reading and analysis. These latter actions will be covered in the next section, but for now we are going to cover actions that can help formulate ideas prior to writing.

### *A. BRAINSTORMING*

We've all been involved in a brainstorming session in one way or another. Simply think back to your elementary school days, when brainstorming was a common lesson involved in English lessons throughout the years. While it may appear to be juvenile—due primarily to us tying the action back to our elementary school days—brainstorming ideas is a very effective action to take before writing. Moreover, brainstorming can be broken down into two broad categories, each of which are rather self-explanatory: brainstorming by group and brainstorming by yourself.

Once you decide to undertake a brainstorming session, there are techniques you can do that help make the session productive. The first technique is commonly referred to as associative brainstorming: take the initial ideas that you have, formulate them into one word phrases, and begin word associations, writing down the first word that comes to mind when seeing the word. This technique is commonly referred to as "word games" or a "word storm" and is particularly efficient at creating new idea streams. Another technique that is useful and intimately tied to the first technique: deconstruction. Deconstructive methodologies, besides being a brainstorming technique, create so many new ideas that an entire school of thought has been constructed around them. Simply take the original idea and rather than breaking it down into its word-by-word basis, you instead approach the idea acting as if you are someone else, reading the sentence in light of their thoughts. For example, you could approach the previous sentence through the lens of a radical feminist, a master technician, or a sophomore art student. Each of these will give you new ideas on where to take the initial idea.

## B. FREE WRITING

Free writing is the action of just writing with no inhibitions. When ideas aren't coming to you, and you need ideas to write on, simply take a piece of paper and a pen, sit down in a quiet area, and just write. Don't worry about the quality of the ideas that come to you, stop thinking about proper grammar, and don't pay attention to your spelling. Just write. When you are done with this—and a good stopping point is when you begin to notice that your writing is slowing down, you are getting tired, or your hand is cramping up—walk away from the writing. Give yourself some time, then go back to the writing. If no new ideas pop out at you at first, take another break. Only give up on the free writing when you have returned three times and can't find any new ideas. At that point you can begin another round of free writing, or move on to other techniques.

## C. QUESTIONING

As you have seen in the previous section, questioning is one of the strongest techniques to utilize while attempting to find new writing ideas. I have already laid out a simple way to do this—asking as many questions as possible and then narrowing them down to common questions—but there are other techniques that can be used to help you come up with useful questions. The one suggestion here is that you should pay attention to what is commonly referred to as "open" and "closed" questions. Closed questions will only provide a simple yes or no answer, while open questions have an infinite possibility of answers. For example, if you ask a closed question like "Are you tired?" you will only get a single answer; if you instead ask "Why are you tired all of the time?" you are bound to get many more possible answers. Always ask open questions to open up new answers, questions, and ideas.

## D. HYPOTHESIZING

Hypothesizing should only be done when you have a series of facts and would like to analyze them. A hypothesis is, essentially, an educated guess that can tie various disparate facts together into a cohesive argument or piece of analysis. Later in the chapter we will cover how to create a strong and effective argument, but in this pre-writing phase we should know that when we have numerous facts, we can begin to create possible guesses on what ties those facts together. Until we learn how to formulate an effective argument, hypothesizing should only be done with caution, as inaccurate guesses can cloud our judgment on what outside evidence is important and what isn't.

## **3. *READING, THINKING, ANALYZING, AND DISCUSSION***

Now that you have whittled down the questions to one or two overarching questions and have begun to formulate a rough direction on where to look to find answers, it is now time to do the actual research portion of the paper. If you are writing a narrative-style piece, particularly one that is fiction, you may be wondering why you would need to even read or research other works if you are making up a story. The following subsection, while on the longer end in terms of length, will detail the strengths of each action in the subsection's title for all types of writing: reading, thinking, analyzing, and discussion.

The first action listed in the subsection's title is reading, and it cannot be understated how important reading is for any type of writing. Reading here can be of two different types, each of which are crucial to your writing. The first is simply reading as much as possible in as many different genres as possible; it should come as no surprise that the best writers are also the best readers. Even if you are writing fiction, reading others' writing will help strengthen your own writing and provide new ideas for writing styles. The second important phase of reading is a more focused reading, a type utilized when beginning the research to find answers to your questions. Knowing the rough, general direction gained from your initial inquiries after narrowing your questions down will allow you to identify and build a bibliography, which can focus your reading to sources more likely to provide answers.

As I have detailed numerous times in the previous paragraphs, reading is beneficial *almost* all the time. Notice that I put the "almost" in italics, as this is for a very good reason. Many people are negligent of reading because they were forced to read through books that are particularly boring reads. Listen, we get it, reading *Moby Dick* or *Ethan Fromm* can be a chore, leading to the common assumption that all books will be a chore. I am here to tell you different, however: books shouldn't be boring. No, this doesn't mean you have to force yourself to like reading; rather, it is no mortal sin to jump around books, genres, and authors. During your general reading, if you can't get past the first 100 pages, put the book down and find something else. Even if, for now, you can't find something that you like, you will still be able to identify the types of writing that you really don't like, which can help you further in writing.

For the purposes of this essay, the remainder of this subsection will detail only those "focused" readings that will help you write each specific style. As such, the next action that can be taken prior to writing is thinking and analyzing, two actions which are so intimately related that they can be hard to differentiate. Here, the two won't be, as the process involved will include both that will help focus your writing. The following then is a simple process that can help you take the focused readings, analyze them, and begin envisioning how it will fit into the overall writing piece.

To begin, prior to starting your focused reading you should develop as strong of a bibliography as possible. Many bibliographies for a wide variety of subjects can be found online, providing you a number of books, journals, and articles that you would not have found on your own. You can also add to the bibliography by finding a book or online article that provides an overview of the field you are looking at and turning to the sources they used. Building a bibliography can be difficult at first, but the more practice you get, the easier it will become as the locations where you can get your sources become more well-known to you.

Once the bibliography is made, you can jump into the reading. It is always a good idea, however, to start with the sources that provide a broad overview of the subject you are researching. Beginning with the broad facts can help frame the reading, creating a link between those sources that can help you in your research. Many online bibliographies and sources that provide broader information will provide that information in an organized manner, often dividing the various readings into "schools" of thought that are often in conversation with each other. Many of these groupings will provide a backbone to the argument that will emerge as your answer. As I have done before as well, if you are planning on writing fiction, the books you will turn to will also be divided into schools, though these categories are based largely on style rather than agreement or opposition.

During your reading, it is best to keep notes that are as organizationally efficient as possible. One method that works really well is to start large—describing each school of thought or style, its common characteristics, and its agreements or disagreements with previous schools of thought or style—then move on to the more general books, moving slowly on to the more specific books over time. In turn, each time you read a more focused book, place it into context within its school of thought and pull out the factors that put it in opposition or agreement with other works in that school and outside it. Keeping these notes organized can help you keep each work in a contextual framework that will be enormously useful in building an argument, an action we will get to later in the paper.

This process includes both analysis and thinking about the books, and places it into a larger framework that can help you understand the entirety of the literature that discusses the specific issue you are examining. Many subjects have specific jargon used to refer to this overall body of literature, phrases that can help you find superb bibliographies online. For example, if you are looking for sources in history, you can explore the "historiography" of a field that describes the entirety of the literature on that subject.

Scientific and social scientific fields often refer to it as the "state of the science." Both of these terms can lead you to excellent lists.

A final note on this section that can help you is the importance of discussion. There is a reason that entire classes, online discussion boards, and meetings are convened to discuss single pieces of writing. While you may have noticed something that you think important, others have not. At the same time, they may have found something that can be crucial to your writing that you overlooked. Discussing a piece of writing with others can bring out answers that you did not think of before. Moreover, what often occurs in these sessions is that multiple overlooked threads of analyses can be synthesized to develop new forms of analyses, something that can help you find novel answers to your questions!

## *4. FINAL STEPS BEFORE WRITING*

At this time, you may have all of your information ready to go to write, but there are still steps you can take to have better quality of writing and to make the actual process of writing easier. These final steps are primarily organizational, in that you will be organizing your thoughts into cohesive notes that will allow you to write without inhibitions. As I have stated before, different writers have different processes they take when preparing to write, actually writing, and editing. The following process, then, can either be followed exactly or you can tweak it to fit your style.

The best technique to first take after gathering the raw information from your reading is to develop an outline. Outlines are a great idea for a variety of reasons, but the biggest reason is that there are no strenuous rules that you have to follow to write an outline. The only thing that has to be remembered when writing an outline is for your main points to be clearly stated, easy to find in the outline, and understandable to you when you walk away from writing. In other words, the outline is meant to make sure you remember main ideas or primary pieces of evidence that you acquired in the reading/research phase. From there, you can have the outline as heavily detailed or sparse as you would like. Whatever fits your style will do!

Another useful technique that can also be used during the previous reading/research phase is a method called "mind mapping." Mind mapping is particularly useful for writers who don't like the linear, organizational style of an outline or think that the outline leaves too many disjointed ideas. Moreover, mind mapping is particularly relevant if you are writing a narrative style of writing or any type of fictional writing. The technique can allow you to develop as many different ideas, characters, events, settings, etc. together in a visual diagram.

To create a mind map, start with the primary question(s) that started you on this path in the first place. Put this in a circle in the middle of a piece of paper and branching from this center circle, place other circles on the outside of the center circle connected by a line. By now, this will look roughly like a spider, with the main question/argument occupying the central circle, and the main points—which will be your main evidentiary points later—as the "legs." From there, you can begin adding subsidiary points to the pieces of evidence or adding extra connections between those points. During many mind mapping sessions, you will come to see that a piece of information you overlooked is more important than you first considered.

As I hinted at above, mind mapping is particularly useful for the narrative form of writing and is particularly helpful in the pre-writing phase of fiction writing. If you are using mind mapping prior to writing fiction, the process is a bit different than simply writing the main argument with primary evidence around it. Mind mapping for fiction is a bit more decentralized, in which you do not start with the main idea in the center of the paper, but start in the four corners: in one corner you write "setting," in another "character," in another you write "plot," and in the final you write "timeline." Rather than doing this mind mapping for the entire book, you do a mind map for each scene, describing the characters, setting, plot, and timeline for each. This gives you a visual representation of each scene and can help you tie together each into a larger picture, from which your writing will emerge whole.

## 5. DRAFTING

We have finally made it to the point where you begin writing the piece. By this point, you should see that the preparation that goes into the pre-writing phase will make this phase the easiest of all steps of writing. Indeed, that preparation, coupled with a robust editing phase, will allow you to write without having to worry about choosing your words specifically or making sure you are grammatically correct at each step. Even with that, however, there are some final tips that should be followed and considered when writing. These primarily deal with structure and will focus your mind to keep your writing as organized as possible so that you do not have to make deep organizational changes during the editing phase.

The first tip that should be considered is the paper's organization. There are numerous ways to organize your writing, but for the purposes of this chapter there are two broad organizational principles that can be applied right now to your writing. These principles are primarily split between nonfiction and fiction writing. In the first, nonfiction, the main point should be written relatively early in as straightforward language as possible, followed by the main ideas or evidence from strongest to weakest. We will get to how to judge the strengths of evidence later in the chapter. The second principle, for fiction writing, is a bit freer: you should make sure the writing flows, in that the plot unfolds in a reasonable manner without any of the writing taking the attention away from the story's merits.

Next we should include a general overview of a good organization for your writing. To put it simply, each nonfiction piece should have an introduction, a "body," and a conclusion. Each can be of varying lengths, depending on the length of the piece: for example, if you are writing a book, your body section will necessarily be multiple chapters, while your introduction and conclusion should only be a chapter each. Regardless of the length of the writing, the body should be the longest section, with the introduction and conclusion being much shorter. As we will get to later, this is for a very good reason: in the body, you have a lot more you have to write, while the introduction and conclusion should be clearly and concisely written.

The next tip is more specific: paragraph structure. As we have learned in the past, a paragraph structure should first start with the topic sentence that introduces a general idea in language that isn't too specific but is still straightforward in language. The topic sentence is general because it will be followed by two or more supporting sentences that further elaborate and explain the topic sentence. You then wrap the paragraph up with a concluding sentence that summarizes the information in the paragraph.

When it comes to paragraph structure, you shouldn't stop at following this blueprint. The first thing that has to be taken into consideration are your transitions. In order to make the reader follow your writing and understand your message, you need to make sure it flows. The best way to ensure the writing flows is through transitional words or phrases that link the paragraphs together. When it comes to writing, making sure the writing flows well, the ideas stay connected and the focus is maintained throughout is paramount to writing as strong a piece as possible.

## *6. EDITING*

The more you write, and the more experience you gain, the more you begin to pick up on certain tips that become natural to your actions as a writer. For many writers that are first starting out, the one area that they overlook is editing, choosing to do a quick read-through after the writing is done to check for common grammatical errors and to make sure that it sounds, to them, like it makes sense. While you should be checking for both, being so flippant about editing and leaving it to one read-through, is a major mistake that many new writers make.

In fact, it is only through multiple runs of editing that your writing becomes better in many different ways. For one, you will begin spotting mistakes in your writing style that can be fixed and avoided in the future. On top of that, you will begin to see excess words and phrases that take away from your message, which you can cut away to make the document more readable. It is little surprise that the best writers in history were also the best critics of their own work: continually editing and re-editing are the actions that turned junk writing into *Ulysses*, *The Old Man and the Sea*, and *Harry Potter*.

With that in mind, the editing phase of writing can be taught and strengthened with practice. More importantly, however, this practice needs to be focused to ensure that you become a top-notch editor of your own work. Editing efficiently can be done in phases, just like the writing process as a whole. Each of the following steps can be, and should be, done multiple times in order to ensure that your writing is as clean as possible. The more you go back and continue revising, the better the writing will be. Finally, even though you may do each phase multiple times, consider going through each phase and then starting at the top rather than doing Phase One three times in a row, Phase Two three times, etc. This will provide you the variety needed to maintain focus.

The first phase of editing is to simply read through the piece. What you should be paying attention to in this first phase is that the main argument or point is communicated clearly and well supported throughout. For fiction pieces, the writing should flow with the characters, setting, plot, and conflicts identifiable and clearly stated. Make sure that throughout the piece, the main and supporting points are well-founded, united together in a flowing narrative, and do not appear disjointed at any point. One of the biggest issues writers face in their writing is a loss of focus at some point during the piece; make sure that every page, section, paragraph, and sentence is absolutely needed to support your main point. If you find a part that appears to be awkward, has chunky writing, or appears to have a part that isn't needed, either cut it or revise it to make it fit better with the overall paper.

The second phase is to check grammar and spelling. In graduate school, I took a course on intelligence, which educated the students to become intelligence analysts in their careers in such agencies as the Central Intelligence Agency, National Security Agency, or Defense Intelligence Agency. As part of the course, our primary assignment was to craft a two-page memo that would, metaphorically, be presented to a high-ranking government official. The theme we had to write on was particularly broad, making the writing and editing particularly grueling as we had to learn to cut out 90% of what we wrote. What we learned, however, was a particularly helpful tip when checking grammar and spelling: instead of reading your paper from start to finish, start at the end *and read backwards*. This forces you to pay attention to what you are reading, essentially compelling you to find mistakes in spelling and grammar that you may have scanned over previously.

Finally, once you have gone through those two phases a couple of times, read through the piece again but take a deconstructive stance. Imagine yourself to be someone else, someone who has a set of beliefs, values, ideas, and worldviews that they will bring to the table when reading, and take another look at your paper. Pay close attention to what critiques pop into your head and take note of them. Walk away from the paper, and instead of re-examining the piece, look at what you wrote and attempt to see if your paper stands successfully on its own in opposition to those points. If it does, keep it; if there is a major hole that you, the writer, are noting on your own writing, go back and further analyze the paper to fix the hole.

As I have mentioned numerous times, editing and proofreading is the most important part of writing. From the vantage point of someone just beginning to write, it seems that professional writers wake up, brew some coffee, eat breakfast, then spew out four Pulitzer Prize-winning articles before dinner, but the truth is far from that. Almost every piece of writing you do, as both an amateur and a professional, you will most likely hate. It only becomes beautiful with editing, that action akin to the taking of a chisel and a block of marble and carving David out of it. Don't skimp on this step. Indeed, spend more time on this than any other.

Throughout this chapter so far, I have aimed to cover, with equal attention, both fiction and nonfiction writing, providing lessons on how to write the various types of writing within each field. The rest of this chapter primarily covers arguments and utilization of outside sources to boost the strength of your writing, but I will conclude with some final notes on how to write both fiction and nonfiction well. The reasoning for this attention bias towards nonfiction is relatively straightforward: detailing how to strengthen the elements of nonfiction writing can be detailed in a chapter, whereas helping with fiction often requires multiple books or classes. If you are looking for more helpful information on writing fiction, I wholeheartedly suggest taking part in a writing class where you can get firsthand experience learning to write.

# *III. Reading and Writing Arguments*

In the world of nonfiction writing, the argument is king. Readers judge the worthiness of a piece of writing based solely on the strength of an argument. In turn, good readers know how to "pick apart" an argument, examining how well evidence supports each other and the primary claim, to judge the veracity of the piece. On the opposite side, the split between a writer and a great writer comes down to the ability to make a clearly stated assertion and support it with evidence that is, in turn, strongly supported itself. While this sounds complicated, breaking down how an argument should be constructed will help you build your own strong arguments, which can be implemented to make a great piece of writing.

Some advice is in line before we jump into deconstructing a strong argument. The aim of this section is to teach you how to both recognize the parts of an argument and teach you how to write a strong argument. Throughout your learning process, it is suggested that you continue to read as much as possible. During the reading, do your absolute best to identify the central assertion, the main points of evidence, and the sub-evidence that supports the evidence. Take note of these, paying attention to how each supports each other and how the author formulates the argument and executes the supporting evidence. Some genres of reading are better than others for beginners to identify arguments, while other genres need a bit more experience to successfully identify the argument. For the beginner, a great location to start are legal cases and pieces of writings detailing actions in the legal world: by the very nature of the job, the argument and evidence have to be clearly stated, allowing the beginner to have a relatively easy time identifying each component. Journal articles are also spectacularly useful, particularly those in the social sciences that explicitly tell you the primary argument in an abstract prior to the main body. On the other hand, many nonfiction books depicting modern politics or more recent history can have arguments that are a bit harder to find; move to these later after practice with the other genres.

The following section will first detail the main components of an argument: the primary assertion and supporting evidence. It will then move on to an examination and explanation of the types of evidence that can be used in an argument, providing examples of these types of evidence in pieces of writing. We will then move on to the section that can be the toughest to understand when first learning about arguments: central assumptions and fallacies. Both of these will have examples to more fully help you understand each and, though they can be difficult to understand, each of these will allow you to better analyze and critique any piece of writing. In turn, it can help you write stronger pieces, with you identifying the central assumptions that go into your thoughts, analyze them, and, in the long run, avoid dangerous assumptions and embrace helpful ones.

## *1. OVERVIEW OF AN ARGUMENT*

The first thing that needs to be stated and pushed out of the way is that an argument in writing and reading is totally different from arguing with someone. An argument is structured, comprised of a main assertion—known, at times, as the conclusion, argument, or assertion—and multiple supporting premises that help "prove" the main assertion. In metaphorical language, arguing is what happens when you come home past your curfew and you and your parents get into a shouting match; an argument is how a lawyer presents a case to a jury, providing evidence to support their claim that an individual should be found guilty or not guilty. As you probably know, these are radically different actions.

The study of arguments is generally undertaken by "logicians," philosophers in numerous different areas that study logic. In turn, logic breaks down an argument into two broad categories, divided by the degree to which the evidence can prove the main assertion. The first category is the deductive argument, which can completely prove—i.e., to 100% with no doubts to the veracity of the statement—a conclusion. Deductive arguments tend to be called "top-down logic," in which a series of general premises, which can be accepted as true, are linked to form a conclusion that can also be taken as true. The most famous example of a deductive argument is the syllogism, a form developed by Aristotle and utilized, in a form written in almost all logic textbooks, as

*If* all men are mortal,

*And*, Socrates is a man

*Then/Therefore*, Socrates is mortal.

We can take the conclusion ("Socrates is mortal") as true because we know both supporting premises are also true. Deductive logic is most notable in modern mathematics, in which a series of evidence that has been proven previously are used together to prove another argument. After years of testing the validity of such an argument—generally by continually testing each piece of evidence and the main assertion in new situations—the assertion can be "proved" to 100%, making a mathematical theory like Newtonian gravity, Einstein's theory of relativity, and the Heisenberg Uncertainty Principle.

The second category of argument is inductive logic. Unlike deductive logic, inductive reasoning cannot prove an assertion to 100% certainty; it can only strongly suggest the veracity of such a statement. It uses a series of evidence, chained together, to supply as strong a proof as possible that the main assertion is true. Thus, the main assertion can only be 99% probable and never 100% true; probability is the key word in inductive arguments. As such, when utilizing an argument in writing, you are more likely than not going to be dealing with inductive logic, building an argument whose assertion and pieces of evidence are strong enough to suggest the veracity of that main argument.

Within each, as referenced repeatedly above, is the main assertion or conclusion. Before we get into the rest of the argument's structure, we should get into how to write a conclusion that can be supported by strong evidence, for if the assertion is faulty, the entire argument will be as well. The argument must be clearly stated, written in language that leaves no doubt as to what the evidence is supporting. Closely linked to the original question(s) you had prior to writing, this clear assertion should utilize strong, active language; it should take a stand on an issue, attempting to convince the reader that your analysis of the facts is correct, and shouldn't be a summary of the facts.

An extension of this assertion is the thesis. Carrying the same principles of the argument, a thesis is a sentence or two that states your argument and then describes how you are going to prove it. In terms of creating a strong piece of writing to support your stance on a given fact, issue, or analyses, utilizing a thesis statement will help you map the paper and maintain the focus of the reader to your claims. Below are two examples, the first being an argument and the second a thesis, taken from my own writing that will help you identify and differentiate both:

- Argument: The federal government's confrontation of organized crime began long before its "wars" of the 1960s-1970s through a series of laws legislated in the 1930s.

- Thesis: In this essay, I argue that the federal government began confronting organized crime long before its major publicized cases against the Italian-American Mafia beginning in the late 1950s and 1960s. By examining pieces of important legislation written and passed between 1932 and 1934, I maintain that these laws served as a foundation from which the federal government confronted organized crime in the 1930s, stopping only with the onset of rising tensions with Nazi Germany and Imperial Japan around 1937.

As you can see, the first argument does not equivocate: I clearly state that the laws passed in the 1930s show the federal government confronting organized crime three decades prior to the more famous confrontations that began in the 1960s. In order to ensure that the reader understands where the essay will go, I provide an overview of the evidence in the thesis statement. This not only helps the reader but makes sure that, in the writing and editing phase, I do not lose sight of the argument. When writing becomes twenty-plus pages, single spaced, it is extremely easy to lose sight. If you are writing a book, this becomes the most common of mistakes.

## *2. EVIDENCE*

After you understand how an argument and thesis works, including how to write it clearly, you move on to the evidence. After the pre-writing phase, you should have large amounts of "data," facts, or story constructions that need to be placed into clear prose. The problem becomes, then, deciding what information is relevant to supporting your main assertion and what can be left out of the writing. This section details, first, deciding what evidence is relevant, moves on then to detail how to judge evidence on its "strength"—or ability to prove the assertion—and ends with how to order the evidence in order to create as strong a case as possible.

Evidence is any piece of information that can be used to support the main assertion. At the heart of an argument is the so-called "burden of proof," both legal or philosophical, that entails an obligation of the individual arguing to give enough supporting evidence of a claim. This jargon is pretty straightforward in laymen's terms: you have to give enough evidence to support your claim in order to get the reader to switch his/her views to your own. In other words, you have to prove your statement; your reader can't do it for you!

Now that we know that it is up to you to find and utilize the best evidence, what types of evidence should you use? This question ultimately shapes how your argument will be communicated; therefore, the type of evidence you find and employ relies most heavily on the audience. As we have noted numerous times throughout the previous section, the audience you are writing for is just as important as the message. In terms of what evidence to include, you should be a careful judge of what types of evidence will resonate most with a certain audience. A great example of this is in political science: if you are familiar with the field, you may notice that the evidence and methodology used are split almost fifty-fifty, between quantitative data and qualitative evidence. While in some cases, such as comparative politics, quantitative data works particularly well, in other areas qualitative evidence works better.

Later we will get to defining and using both primary and secondary sources, but for now suffice it to say that there are strengths to using both. If you are writing a piece of original research in the humanities, social science, and/or law, utilizing primary sources can bolster your argument exponentially. Other fields have uses for primary sources, but these three tend to be where they are most useful. Secondary sources, on the other hand, can be used for any type and genre of writing. Indeed, knowing the literature on the subject, whether you plan on using the source as evidence or not, will be helpful to your writing.

The only item left to cover is what constitutes strong evidence. The "strength" of a piece of evidence lies closely intertwined with that "burden of proof" mentioned above, in that evidence can be either a direct proof or circumstantial evidence. The former, direct proof, is a piece of evidence, or multiple pieces of evidence put together, that proves the veracity of a conclusion. Circumstantial evidence, on the other hand, can prove a conclusion to a variety of degrees, but can never prove an assertion with absolute certainty.

Before we move on to the next subsection, a provision of examples of these two types of evidence are in order. Direct proof of an assertion, while decently self-explanatory, are pieces of evidence that cannot be disproven. A piece of direct proof is a video shot, in high definition, of an individual robbing a house and, in the midst of their stealing session, they look right at the camera. Discounting the possibility of an "evil twin" and taken together with that individual's fingerprints all over the house, this is direct proof of guilt. Circumstantial, on the other hand, are items like fingerprints alone, the word of the suspect's acquaintance that said he planned on robbing a house the night of the robbery, or the fact that the neighbor saw the same model and colored car outside of the house at the time of robbery. Alone, they do not sufficiently prove the conclusion that the individual is the one who committed the crime; taken together, however, it can sufficiently prove the conclusion.

## *3. PUTTING IT TOGETHER: HOW TO CONSTRUCT A STRONG ARGUMENT*

Now that you have learned what the central assertion is, how it operates, and how you should write it, and have learned what evidence is, how to use it, and what constitutes direct and circumstantial evidence, we have to be able to put it all together to communicate an efficient argument. The best way to take argument, evidence, and sub-evidence into a flowing general argument is to use the Toulmin Method. This method was named after its developer, British philosopher Stephen Toulmin, and is a way to organize reasoning into a coherent whole to prove an assertion. Each of the major parts needed in an argument are included, with the method providing a basis for the components to support and be supported by each other.

Before we get into *how* to write using the Toulmin Method, it is a good idea to cover its components, most of which you will know from our discussion above with a few added elements that will further strengthen your writing. The Toulmin Method begins first with the item we have already discussed: the primary assertion, or "claim" as the method calls it. This is both the central assertion or thesis statement that the author is trying to prove. The last recognizable item is the inclusion of what Toulmin refers to as "data" but we know as evidence. Thus the first two items included in the Toulmin Method are the two we have already discussed in detail above, so we don't have to go into more detail here.

Yet there are four other parts included in the method that need to be discussed prior to showing you how to write the argument: the warrant/bridge, backing, counterclaim, and rebuttal. Following the evidence, the method includes what is called the "warrant" or "bridge," which is an analysis on how the evidence you provided supports the argument and any underlying assumptions that tie the evidence and argument together. Next is the "backing" or "foundation" which is just an inclusion of any reasoning that might be needed to help support the warrant; if the bridge needs outside reasoning to explain how the evidence and conclusion are tied together, you provide that here. The last of the extra items are the counterclaim and rebuttal, which is the presentation of a claim that opposes your assertion and then uses your evidence or other evidence to show that your assertion is correct while the opposing view is incorrect; this balances your argument and shows that you considered the opposing view.

The Toulmin Method should first be laid in outline form, laying out each of these items beginning first with the claim, then the data, the bridge, the backing (if necessary), the counterclaim, and ending with the rebuttal. The actual writing can put these in any order, but to maintain the flow of the paper it is actually better to make sure that the order you used in the outline isn't used in the paper. The remainder of this section details the best way to construct the paper to fully draw out the argument.

First, as we detailed earlier in the section on the parts of a paper that need to be included, we can begin with the introduction. In the introduction section, begin first with an introductory paragraph or two; many writers will begin with a short anecdote that summarizes, symbolizes, or shows an actual manifestation of your argument in the world. You then move on to clearly stating your argument or thesis, writing how you are going to prove your argument through a general overview of the evidence you have. Here, you shouldn't get too specific on the evidence, as the evidence should be fully drawn out in the body. Before you wrap up the introduction section, you should include the counterclaim, detailing how your argument differs from the argument of your opponent(s). This can help more fully draw out your argument, showing how it differs from other arguments and, ultimately, how it contributes to the overall literature.

The next section is the body. Broadly speaking, you should have your evidence and any sub-evidence that support the evidence included here. However, the most important aspect of the body should actually be the bridge. Evidence stated alone can be too disjointed, providing an argument and evidence with no discernible connections between them. Rather than only including the bridge in a few paragraphs at the end of the body section, you should instead intersperse bridge paragraphs between the pieces of evidence. Indeed, each time evidence is utilized in the piece, you should make the conscious effort to tie each piece to each other and show how that supports the argument. Moreover, the bridge ensures that the interpretation you made with the information—which essentially created your argument—is the same interpretation the reader will get.

Finally, we move to the concluding section which generally wraps the paper up but can be more than simply giving concluding remarks. Here, you should bring back the counterclaim that was first written in the introduction and utilize your evidence and bridge information to argue against it. By this point, if the assertion, evidence, and bridge are clearly articulated, your reader should be able to see clearly how the opposing argument is discounted. Regardless, you should clearly detail why the evidence supports your assertion over the claims of the opposing side. In doing so, this will conclude your writing better than simple remarks as it keeps the lines of communication open for another writer to enter the argument as well.

## *4. READING ARGUMENTS*

The next step toward learning arguments is being able to read others' arguments and fully comprehend them. A bit of a warning: learning to recognize arguments in others' writing can be very difficult, particularly when the author doesn't clearly state their argument. However, this difficulty in no way should prevent you from learning how to identify another writer's argument, as there are tips that can help you identify arguments, evidence, etc. and be able to comprehend the entirety of the writing. The number one action to take in order to be able to identify arguments each time you read is to practice by reading as much as possible. The more you actively read, looking for the argument and identifying the main assertion and evidence, the more easily you will be able to identify and analyze a writer's argument.

A great way to identify an argument quickly is to first glance through the writing. If it is an article, scan through the writing, reading the headings, introduction paragraphs to each, and introduction and conclusion sentences of the paragraphs. If it is a book, read the blurb; look at the chapter titles, paying attention to which chapters are longer in length; flip to the index, quickly scanning through to see what terms are important by the amount of times they are used throughout the book. In this initial reading, you aren't supposed to know what the piece is about; instead, you are using this initial reading to get a general idea of what the author is talking about. Gathering these clues can allow you to begin reading with a general idea of where the argument will land in the overall literature. Knowing this information will help you identify the argument.

Now you can begin your reading, actively paying attention to a number of factors including the central argument, the core pieces of evidence, any counter-arguments, and how the author ties together evidence and argument with the bridge. It is here that you can attempt to find the stated argument, and there are tips to do so instead of just searching randomly. First, consider the context: in your initial read-through, what broad ideas popped out at you as important? If certain ideas did seem important, keep an eye out for the statements by the author discussing that idea.

From there, keep an eye out for argument indicator words or phrases, such as "I argue," "I assert," "therefore," and others. Be careful here! Some authors use the phrase "As opposed to_____ (other author)," or "While_____ argues this, it appears that…" Neither of these are thesis or argument indicators, but indicators of an opposing view. While this information can be a part of the argument, it is not the entirety of it. Oftentimes, when authors use this tactic, you will have to use the information in the sentences around it to formulate your own idea of what the author is arguing. While this can be frustrating to do, and ultimately takes away from the stance of the author, it is still written in a better narrative flow that many authors choose to sacrifice clarity for flow.

## 5. JUDGING THE STRENGTH OF AN ARGUMENT

The final item that needs to be elaborated before ending this section is how to judge the strength of an argument. Since you can read and identify others' arguments and can construct your own in writing, it is particularly helpful to know what makes a strong argument to judge both your own writing and the validity of others' arguments. If, when you are writing and editing your own piece you can recognize what is a strong argument and what isn't, you can fix this in the editing phase, which can help you craft strong arguments each and every time. As a writer with years of experience, I can tell you that being able to judge the strength of an argument can help you in the pre-writing, writing, and editing phases so much that it will save you headaches later.

If you Google search "strong arguments" the results can be divided roughly into two categories: the strength of an argument in terms of logic, and the strength of an argument in terms of its ability to convince. While the former is worthwhile to learn—judging the strength of an argument by its ability to follow set logical formulas—it is not what will be covered here. Rather, we will be discussing the strength of arguments by its ability to prove its conclusion. Judging the strengths of arguments in this way depends on the clearness of the central assertion, the quality of the evidence you utilized, and how well you link the pieces of evidence together with the main assertion in your bridge.

The first indication of a strong argument is a clearly written and articulated conclusion or central assertion. The clearness of an argument is dependent not just on its ability to be readily understood by the reader, but also on its ability to identify, confront, and elaborate on the core assumptions that could be driving that assertion. Assumptions, by nature, are generally hidden, but in order to ensure the integrity of the argument, these assumptions need to be brought to the light so that they are not used to discount the argument. When your assertion is clearly written, and the assumptions that drive it are brought to the light—either directly or indirectly—the assertion will be strengthened.

Next, the evidence you used—and why you decided on that specific evidence—needs to be reasonably chosen, should clearly support your stance, and shouldn't lose focus in the writing. As stated above, strong evidence can be taken from both secondary and primary sources and needs to be chosen with the audience in mind. The evidence you do choose to utilize needs to be in a specific order, from strongest to weakest and, in ordering them, remember to buttress the weaker arguments to make sure it doesn't take away from the strength of the argument. Finally, the inclusion of evidence and any additional support for that evidence cannot lose sight of the main assertion; losing focus causes the reader to forget what the argument was. Taken together, you can remember these tips for evidence when writing; when reading, question whether the evidence used helps support the author's argument and whether the focus is maintained throughout (you will notice if the focus is lost as you will begin forgetting what the argument is).

The final and most important aspect in judging the strength of an argument is the bridge. A conclusion and evidence presented in the proper order is little more than a mathematical equation. In order to show how the evidence supports other pieces of evidence, the central assertion, and the argument as a whole, the analysis needs to be strong. Rudimentary evidence or raw data can appear to be weak until the writer puts their specific spin and analysis on those facts. A true master of this was French philosopher Michel Foucault, who was able to take common, mundane evidence and, through his analysis, show the existence of Western "thought systems" was absolute genius. Indeed, from a common history of psychological disorders in Europe from the 1400s on, Foucault was able to uncover systems of power radically different from our previous perceptions. This is the reason the bridge is so important.

Ultimately, in writing and reading arguments, you should be asking yourself a series of questions to ensure that the argument is strong. Does the evidence support the conclusion? Do any pieces of evidence appear to be disjointed, as if they don't belong in the overall argument or do not appear to be needed? Do you forget what the assertion is when reading? Are all of the pieces of evidence adequately explained and make clear linkages between each other and the conclusion? If so to all of these, the argument is strong. If not, and you are the writer, go back and plug these holes to make sure the argument's integrity is strong.

### 6. ROTTENBERG METHOD

The Rottenberg method is based on Annette Rottenberg's adjustments to Stephen Toulmin's model of argument. The Rottenberg method structure is comprised of three parts:
- Claim
- Support
- Warrant

Unlike Toulmin's model, which is biased toward logical appeals, Rottenberg confronts this bias and includes:

- Motivational appeals. A warrant "based on appeals to the needs and values of an audience, designed to evoke an emotional response"

- Audience-centered approach. An argument that is not only logical but will win the reader over to your stated point of view.

## IV. Sources: Where to Find Information, Evaluate, and Cite in Paper

While the information in this section could have been included in the section detailing how to research and find information effectively, it seems best to provide an entire section on sources that come after the argument section. This is for a very good reason: once you understand what you are looking for to build and execute a strong argument, understanding what sources to turn to will be easier to understand. As such, the two primary areas of sources that you will be turning to are either primary or secondary sources, though we will only be covering secondary sources here, as primary sources—sources written in a specific historical time period that can help provide evidence of that period—are only used in history. On top of this information will be sections on how to evaluate the legitimacy/strength of a source, how to use those sources in your writing, and how to properly cite those documents. Take a deep breath and jump in! You're almost done!

## *1. SECONDARY SOURCES OVERVIEW*

A secondary source is any document, video, or recording that details and analyzes information that appears first in a primary source—a source that is created during the same period that the event is occurring. This definition can be dubious, however, as a book that was published during a specific historical time period that reflects that period's *zeitgeist* is a primary source, though it may be discussing events that they read in another primary source. The safest way to remember the difference between a secondary source and a primary source is that if the author did not witness the events portrayed, it is a secondary source. Since we are paying attention to how to use sources for nonfiction writing, paying attention to the differences between the types of both sources matter only for citations, which we will get to later.

The most commonly used secondary source utilized by writers are scholarly books and articles in peer-reviewed journals. For scholarly books, there are two primary sources from which books can be found: mass market publishers and university publishers. While the former tends to promote books that are easier to read, it is often more difficult to identify the argument in these books as the publisher makes sure the book reads well. University published books are more scholarly, straightforward writing that attempts to maintain clarity throughout. Both places are great to find sources for your work.

Peer-reviewed journals are also great places to find sources. These academic journals can be great sources of both articles that relate to your argument or reviews of books that can help you find works relevant to your writing. Academic journals are great resources due to the intensity of the review process taken: the "peer-review" means that the article, prior to being published, has been reviewed and edited in multiple rounds by experts in the field. This review process creates articles that are factually accurate and are able to create productive conversations in the future.

## *2. EVALUATING SECONDARY SOURCES*

Knowing what sources will help you in your research can be difficult to surmise, as is evidenced by the difficulties seen in knowing the difference between a primary and secondary source. However, once you move past those initial difficulties and move instead to choose sources that can work for your research, there are tips that can help guide you in finding the right sources. Finding the right ones involves a mix between judging the source before you interact with it and judging it prudently after the interaction. Doing so both prior to and after interacting with the source multiple times will become habit, with you eventually doing it subconsciously to each source you come into contact with.

Before we get into the steps that you can take both before and after interacting with sources, it is best to get a general rule out of the way that will help you regardless of the type of source. You should always turn first to newer sources, saving older sources for later. When I write "newer sources" here I do not necessarily mean those sources that came out within the past year: sources up to twenty-years-old for some genres will be perfectly acceptable to use. The general rule of thumb is that if you are working in the humanities, books going back to the early 1990s can be used and relied upon; for the social sciences, political science and law in particular, you should only be using sources stretching back to the early 2000s; for science literature, be very careful when using sources that are older than ten years, as many of the facts could have been proven or disproven since.

When first encountering a source, there are two primary things you can do to judge the quality of the source and whether it will work well for you in writing: reading reviews and doing a first read-through. In the first, almost every type of source available has a review somewhere on the market. For sources that are more recent, check out newspapers to find reviews: major newspapers like *The New York Times*, *The Washington Post*, *Los Angeles Times*, or *Chicago Tribune* all have excellent reviews. Simply run the title of the source through Google and read through some of the reviews. You should get a couple of results that can give you an idea of what the source is arguing before you interact with it.

At the same time, some sources will not have reviews in newspapers. In particular, when you are going to use sources from either an academic source or a source that is not even a year old yet, reviews may not be available. In these cases, go to the book's page on the publisher's website to read a short overview of the argument to get a rough idea of what the source can offer. After you have done this, you can move on to the next possible action before interacting with the source.

This final step is to do the initial read through that I suggested earlier when discussing how to find an argument in others' writing. As I detailed before, you will want to begin by first examining the source's blurb, table of contents, and index to get a general idea of what the source is conveying. Next, take some time to read the introduction to fully understand what the argument is, combining what you learned here with what you discovered in the blurb, table of contents, and index. From there you can begin to form a judgment on whether the source will work for you.

Judging how well the source will work for you after interacting with it requires a mixture of subjective judgment, weighing how well it supports your assertion, and judging how credible the source is. In this case, the subjective judgment is a fancy way of saying that you have to make a decision whether the source is useful to you, then make a decision on how well it can be used as a supporting device for your argument. This leads us to the third requirement: judging how credible the source is. Credibility of a source can be found in numerous ways, but the most important is to look at reviews of the source and examine the citations used in the book. If the argument is strong, is supported by factually correct evidence, and that evidence is supported with numerous references, the source is strong. Reviews will also tell you whether the source has pitfalls that you need to keep in mind when judging the source.

These steps will ultimately help you judge the usefulness and credibility of sources. As I mentioned above, your tactics to evaluating a source will grow better with more practice. Utilizing these methods both prior to and following the interaction with a source will eventually become natural, allowing you to do so without having to follow a "checklist" of sorts. More importantly, however, the sources that you decide to use in your paper, if you utilize these tactics, will make sure the sources you use are supportive of your argument.

## *3. USING SOURCES*

Once you know what sources to go with and how to judge those sources' credibility, you are going to need to know how to use those sources within the text itself. There are three ways you can use the source in the writing itself, all of which need to be properly cited—which we will get to in the next section—and that are used interchangeably throughout most texts. This latter statement means that you shouldn't utilize only one tactic of including other sources, but use all of them to get the ideas from that source communicated efficiently. Indeed, as you will find when writing, you may not be able to summarize or paraphrase a source's argument efficiently so you will need to quote it, either shortly or within a block text.

The first tactic in using the information garnered from a source within the text is to summarize. The first to thing to know when planning on summarizing a text is that it should be brief. A summary of a text should be, at most, a paragraph. Within this summary, you should include the source's argument, any "between the lines" assumptions, and your own analysis of the source. By using the summary in such a way as to tie it in with your own argument or evidence will allow the reader to understand that both your main assertion and evidence are well supported throughout the literature without having to include lengthy quotes.

Even shorter still is paraphrasing a source. Paraphrasing involves only a sentence or two detailing the primary ideas used in that source, be it the general ideas communicated from the source or the source's argument. Paraphrasing should be no longer than two sentences and is generally used next to other statements paraphrasing other sources. In general, most pieces of writing will use paraphrasing in the sections describing the historiography or state of the science, or within the section that details the counterviews that will be argued against.

Yet for those texts where summaries and paraphrasing doesn't work, you should consider quoting the source. Quoting sources has many benefits, but the most important is the fact that the reader will be able to see that the source is saying what you are claiming it is saying. There are two ways to use quotations within text: in-text quotations and block quotes. To use quotes in-text, choose a sentence from the source that encapsulates the idea you want communicated and place it in quotes, breaking the quotes up with short bits of analysis if the quote is unclear. The other way to use quotations is to utilize the block quote, which takes a sample from the sources text and places it within your text. The text should be set apart from your writing by setting the indent one inch farther from the margins than your text. Within these block quotes, you can use ellipses if the sentences you want to include from the source are too spaced apart. With that in mind, make sure the block quote runs to only six to eight lines at max, or you will lose the interest of the reader.

## *4. CITING AND DOCUMENTING*

Efficiently citing and documenting the sources you use in your paper is one of the most important things you need to do when writing. Not citing or improperly citing the documents you used is not just wrong, but in many cases it can be illegal. Ultimately, what you are doing is ascribing ideas to those who "own" them, or wrote them; if you fail to do so, you are stealing ideas. Therefore, the more sources you include, the more you should be citing. On top of these questions of legality, it must also be remembered that properly citing sources will make your paper stronger and more believable to the reader.

The first item we are going to cover here are the three popular documentation styles—MLA, APA, and Chicago—and the strengths in choosing each. The first documentation style is the MLA, which stands for the Modern Language Association; it is used primarily for papers written in the liberal arts or humanities. As we will discuss with the other documentation styles, the MLA has specific guidelines on how the paper should be written: these guidelines can be found online. Moreover, with each type of documentation, there are ways that you have to cite each type of source and these differ between in-text and the citations used in bibliographies.

We can begin first with the in-text citations. The MLA stylebook requires that you utilize parentheses in order to properly cite the material. The parentheses used will include the author, page number and, if you are using more than one work from one author, the year it is published. For example, if you were using a source like Benjamin Franklin's autobiography, you would quote as:

- "In 1732 I first published my Almanack [sic], under the name of *Richard Saunders*; it was continu'd [sic] by me about twenty-five years, commonly call'd *Poor Richard's Almanac*" (169).

Notice a few things about the quote above. First, I used the phrase *sic* in brackets: this is a Latin phrase used throughout writing to indicate that the way you quoted the text, with all of its quirks in spelling and grammar, is how it appears in the original source. Moreover, in this case I am using only one quote from Franklin's *Autobiography*: if I were to use more than one book written by Franklin, I would write (Franklin, 1749, 33) in addition to (Franklin, 1793, 169) for the *Autobiography* source. If you find two or more sources from the same author that are written during the same year, you use an alphabetical sequence to indicate the order of publication. For example, if John Smith wrote four essays in 2016 that you quoted, you would indicate them as (Smith, 2016a, 43), (Smith, 2016b, 10), and so on. Finally, if you write that "according to [author]…" you do not have to put the author's name in the quotations, including only the year and page number.

The MLA also requires a works cited page. First, you make a separate page and title it "Works Cited." Next, you take each source you cited and, in alphabetical order, cite them according to the following rules. Each type of source has specific rules, but if you follow these guidelines, you will be documenting them correctly:

- Book: Last Name, First Name. *Title*. Publisher, Publication Date.
    - o   For example: Franklin, Benjamin. *The Autobiography of Benjamin Franklin*. Henry Holt and Company, 1916.
- Journal: Last Name, First Name. "Title of Article." *Title of Journal*, Volume, Issue, Year, page numbers.
    - o   For example: Smith, John. "The Intricacies of Citation." *American Citation History*, 17, 1, 2016, 114-151.
- Magazine: Last Name, First Name. "Title." *Periodical Title*, Day Month Year, pages.
    - o   For example: White, Henry. "Mr. Grammar Nazi Comes to Town." *Grammar Daily*, 20 Feb. 2014, pp. 80-84.
- Newspaper: Last Name, First Name. "Title." *Publication*, Day Month Year, page.
    - o   For example: Que, John. "Grammar Police Hold Two in Thievery: More Arrests to Come Says Chief." *The Buffalo Quotidian*, 24 Mar 2002, p. A1.

Though the MLA does utilize other ways to cite other sources, these are the most commonly cited.

Next up is the APA, which stands for the American Psychological Association. As can be seen from the name, APA citation is generally used by the social sciences and uses specific page modifications just as the MLA does. Much like the MLA as well, the APA has specific guidelines for both in-text citations and documentation at the end of the document. As we did with the MLA guide—and will do with Chicago—we will start here with in-text citations before moving on to the citation page. Here, I can only describe how to cite the most used types of sources, but you can find more information online by running a Google search of APA documentation style.

In-text citations in the APA style are similar to MLA's in-text citation in that they utilize parentheses to cite the author. The difference here is that the APA style guide suggests that you always lead the quotation with a phrase that includes the author's name, such as "According to Smith…" These include both short and block quotations, with the latter being led by a phrase much like that above, ended with a colon. Following the quotation, you must use parentheses that follows an order much like the MLA: author (if you cannot include in the leading statement), date (if an author has multiple sources in the same year, use a, b, c, and so on after the year), and page number. Below, I have included both a short quote and a block quote to illustrate these rules.

- Short quote: According to Franklin, in 1754 he "projected and drew a plan for the union of all the colonies under one government, so far as might be necessary for defense, and other important general purposes" (1916, p. 241).

- Block quote: Franklin's (1916) recollection of the Albany Plan is telling:

    o In our way thither, I projected and drew a plan for the union of all the colonies under one government, so far as might be necessary for defense, and other important general purposes. As we pass'd [sic] thro' [sic] New York, I had shown my project to Mr. James Alexander and Mr. Kennedy…and, being fortified by their approbation, I ventur'd to lay it before the Congress. It then appeared that several commissioners had form'd plans of the same kind. (p. 241)

As we did with the MLA, there are a few things that should be pointed out. First, for the shorter quotes, you should end the sentence with the quotation, then include the parenthetical citation, followed by the period. Second, the block quotes should be single space with ½ inch margins like the MLA guide. Finally, for the block quote, the leading statement must include the author's name followed by the year of publication: in this case, it is "Franklin (1916)."

For the works cited page begin first on a separate page at the end of the essay labeled "References" that should be centered on the top of the page. Next, the authors should be listed alphabetically, last name first and first name following. From there, some items will look familiar to you, but others are new. Pay attention to how each is documented for each type of source:

- Book: Last name, first name initial (publication year). *Title: First letter in subtitle also capitalized.* Publisher location: Publisher.
    - o   For example: Smith, J. (2012). *Grammar and APA Citation.* New York: Grammar School Publications.

- Edited book: Last name, first name initial (Eds.). (publication year). *Title.* Publisher location: Publisher.
    - o   For example: Smith, J. & Doe, J. (Eds.). (2012). *APA In Action.* New York: Grammar School Publications.

- Journal article organized by Volume: Last name, first name initial. (Year). Article title. *Journal title, Volume number,* pages.
    - o   For example: Smith, J. (2001). Critique and Analysis of the APA. *Journal of Documentation and Citation, 41,* 401-439.

- Journal article organized by Issue: Last name, first name initial. (publication year). Article title. *Journal title, volume (issue),* pages.
    - o   For example: Smith, J. (2004). From MLA to APA: The Woes of Switching Documentation Style. *American Journal of Citation, 10(2),* 5-32.

- Magazine article: Last name, first name initial. (year, month day). Title. *Magazine title, issue number,* pages.
    - o   For example: Smith, J. (2005, January 3). When students kill: Why a murder happened over proper documentation style. *Newsweek, 244,* 30-36.

- Newspaper article: Last name, first name initial. (year, month day). Title. *Newspaper*, page number(s).
    - o   For example: Smith, J. (1999, May 1). State calls for standardized citation guide. *The Belmont Times,* p. 1A.

We can now move on to the Chicago citation, which can be used across the board in terms of scholarly field. The Chicago citation guide is used by a wide array of writer for two very good reasons: it is extremely easy to use and it does not stop the flow of writing. As we did with both the MLA and APA citations and documentations, we will start with the in-text citations—which are radically different from both the MLA and APA—and end with the works-cited page.

Chicago citation and documentation utilizes the footnote or endnote to cite sources. Footnotes or endnotes are really useful for citing within the document, as you simply choose to insert a reference that gives you a small number above the desired location that can still be seen but doesn't stop the flow of writing or reading. To insert a footnote on a Word document, you click "Insert," then footnote, at which time the number will be placed at the location where you placed your cursor and will open a space at the bottom for the reference corresponding to the number. The footnote style uses the following style:

- Books: First name last name, *Title* (Place of publication: Publisher, year of publication), page number.
  - For example: John Smith, *Chicago Citation* (New York: Grammar School Publications, 2013), 14-26.
- Journal article: First name last name, "Title of Article," *Journal Title* Volume, issue number (year): page number.
  - For example: John Smith, "A Critique of Chicago Citation," *American Journal of Citation* 42, no. 3 (2004): 621-667.
- Magazine: Author name, "Title," Magazine title, Month year, page number.
  - For example: John Smith, "The Return of the Grammar Nazi," Newsweek, February 2003, 34-37.
- Online magazine: Author name, "Title," *Magazine title*, Month day, year, URL.
  - For example: John Smith, "Is the President Willing to Change Grammar Rules?" *Citation Daily*, May 1, 2014, http://www.citationdaily.com
- Newspaper: Author name, "Title," *Newspaper* (Location of newspaper), Month day, year.
  - For example: John Smith, "President Weighs in on Grammar Rules," *Bellefontaine Bee* (Bellefontaine, OH), Jan. 11, 2011.

The works cited page utilizes guidelines that are remarkably similar to the MLA and APA style guides, and similar to what is used in the footnotes. For the sake of brevity, I will forego the individual examples here as the rules for the documentation page are almost the same as the footnotes. Begin first with a separate page at the end of the document and label it "Bibliography," centered at the top of the page. Then, in alphabetical order by the sources authors' last name, list the sources you used following the same guidelines as the footnotes. For example, rather than write the footnote over again in the bibliographic page, you begin first with the last name followed by the first name separated by a comma. After each subsequent entry (source title, magazine/journal/newspaper title, date, etc.) you use a period rather than a comma. Finally, you do not include any parentheses for publication location, publisher name, or date. Here are just two examples of bibliographic entries as they should appear on your paper:

- Smith, John. *Chicago Citation.* New York: Grammar School Publications, 2012.
- Smith, John. "A Critique of Chicago Citation." *American Journal of Citation* 42, no. 3. 2004.

Before we conclude the paper, just a few more items need to be pointed out. First, you only use the page numbers in the footnote entries, never in the bibliography. Second, when your bibliographic entry runs longer than one line, you indent the second line and any subsequent lines needed after. Finally, though I did not do this here, each time the bibliographic entry runs longer than two lines, you should single-space it, utilizing double spacing between each entry. The final two help the reader read the entries and differentiate them from each other.

# V. Conclusion

Now that you have read through this lengthy chapter, it is my hope that you have learned a little more about writing. It is a hope that you have some knowledge that will allow you to go forth, read, write, and experiment and just create. The bottom line here is that writing, while at times a complex process, is creation, a core characteristic of the human condition. And just like other facets of the human condition—love, thought, beliefs, and ideals—writing can be built with continued practice.

Indeed, a great professor once told me that great writers are not born naturally talented. They are born tenacious, unwilling to give up, and willing to continue chiseling away until their skills become expertise. At the same time, just like other skills that you can learn and master over your lifetime, the practice you undertake to write has to be focused, building skills necessary to become a great writer and recognizing and fixing those mistakes you may be committing. Both of these can be done by writing with others, in groups that can help critique your writing and make you into a greater writer.

At the same time, and as a final word, you should be reading as much as humanly possible. It is an oft-cited unattributed quote that the best writers are also the best readers. When essayist and writer Christopher Hitchens passed away in 2011, many writers, in their memoirs of the man, commented on how great a reader he was. When you read his writing, this is the most recognizable aspect, in which Hitchens' amazingly clear voice breaks through in writing that masterfully critiques and analyzes literature. Hitchens was not alone in this: if you read any book from the assortment of award-winning nonfiction works, you will notice that the author's ability to critique and analyze other works are masterful.

Thus we come to the end of our chapter, and a summary of this conclusion, to provide a checklist of sorts, is in order. The more you read and the more you write, focusing on better writing and fixing your mistakes, the better your writing will be. When doing this, never give up: set yourself a daily writing amount—say, 1,000 words a day—and stick to that schedule, writing every single day. Finally, take the tips I have laid out for you in identifying arguments to make yourself a better reader, able to recognize arguments to more fully understand others' writings. I hope to one day see your writing!

## Sample Test Questions

1) The _____ type of writing aims to educate the reader on a certain topic.

    A) Informative
    B) Argumentative
    C) Narrative
    D) Critical response
    E) Persuasive

The correct answer is A:) Informative. An informative essay aims to do just that: inform the reader or audience of a specific matter.

2) A longer book or piece of writing can combine _____ types of writing together.

    A) Narrative and persuasive
    B) Critical response and informative
    C) All five
    D) No two
    E) Argumentative and informative

The correct answer is C:) all five. In many longer books, the writer will utilize all five forms of writing to effectively communicate their message.

3) The _____ form of writing can be the most flexible form of writing that can be used in numerous different situations.

   A) Persuasive
   B) Critical response
   C) Informative
   D) Narrative
   E) Argumentative

The correct answer is D:) Narrative. The narrative form of writing can be utilized in numerous different areas and can provide a framework to implement other forms of writing in longer pieces.

4) The _____ type of writing aims to lay out and support a key conclusion or assertion.

   A) Critical response
   B) Persuasive
   C) Narrative
   D) Informative
   E) Argumentative

The correct answer is E:) Argumentative. As the name suggests, the argumentative form of writing seeks to articulate an argument and support it through strong evidence.

5) The _____ type of writing aims to persuade the reader to think in a certain manner or take a certain action.

   A) Critical response
   B) Persuasive
   C) Narrative
   D) Argumentative
   E) Informative

The correct answer is B:) Persuasive. While this answer may seem pretty obvious—a persuasive piece of writing aiming to persuade—what is not obvious is that persuasive writing can be found in a wide array of writing types, including books, articles, essays, and even advertisements.

6) One form of persuasive writing called a _____ aims to convince a political leader to adopt a certain view or take a certain action.

   A) Essay
   B) Memo
   C) Presidential Daily Briefing
   D) Congressional Briefing
   E) Note

The correct answer is B:) Memo. While the Presidential Daily Briefing and Congressional Briefing are specific types of memos, the questions asks for a broader category. Thus, any document written expressly for a particular politician to persuade them to take a certain action or adopt a certain view is a memo.

7) The _____ type of writing responds to another writer's argument.

   A) Informative
   B) Argumentative
   C) Critical response
   D) Persuasive
   E) Narrative

The correct answer is C:) Critical response. A critical response takes another writer's piece and responds to it by developing another argument in which the evidence opposes the evidence in the other writer's argument.

8) Another name that is commonly used to refer to the informative writing is the _____ essay.

   A) Expository
   B) Narrative
   C) Explanatory
   D) Formative
   E) Critical response

The correct answer is A:) Expository. In many cases, writers will refer to informative writing as an "expository essay."

9) The _____ type of writing is always nonfiction.

   A) Informative
   B) Argumentative
   C) Narrative
   D) Persuasive
   E) Critical response

The correct answer is B:) Argumentative. While the other forms of writing can be utilized in fiction writing, writing an argumentative piece should always be nonfiction.

10) When writing, you _____ follow the writing order depicted in the chapter.

   A) Absolutely have to
   B) Don't have to
   C) Maybe have to
   D) Might want to
   E) Might not want to

The correct answer is B:) Don't have to. It is absolutely not necessary to follow the order laid out in the chapter for pre-writing, writing, and editing. In fact, most writers approach writing through a variety of approaches and the process depicted here is only a helpful method that can guide you through the writing process.

11) The best method to take in pre-writing is to simply _____.

   A) Research
   B) Read
   C) Question
   D) Steal ideas from others
   E) Re-write something you've written before

The correct answer is C:) Question. It is suggested that you begin first by asking as many questions as possible, walking away from it, then returning to try to spot questions that are asking the same thing. These edited questions should be the ones you use to begin the writing process.

12) Before getting into the writing, you should take the questions you formulated and go to the _____ to get an idea of where you should begin looking to get answers.

   A) Teacher
   B) Encyclopedia
   C) IRS
   D) Internet
   E) Guru of knowledge

The correct answer is D:) Internet. While it may be possible to consult a teacher or an encyclopedia, simply running your question through an internet search engine like Google or Bing will provide you with results that will help begin your exploration.

13) If you can't find writing ideas from questioning, you can _____, either by group or by yourself.

   A) Give up
   B) Throw it away
   C) Free write
   D) Brainstorm
   E) Quit school

The correct answer is D:) Brainstorm. Brainstorming can provide numerous ideas for your writing, and can be completed either by yourself or in a group. In both cases, the tactics to effectively brainstorm are similar, designed to get you and/or your group to come up with workable ideas rather quickly.

14) One technique to effectively brainstorm is _____ brainstorming, which formulates ideas from single words.

   A) Associative
   B) Word games
   C) Word storm
   D) Deconstruction
   E) Additional

The correct answer is A:) Associative. Associative brainstorming begins first with you, the writer, coming up with a single word. Once it is written down, you write down the first word that comes to mind when thinking of that word. Continue this until an idea comes together. While A is the correct answer here, both B and C are other names for associative brainstorming.

15) The _____ method involves approaching ideas in the mindset of another individual.

   A) Additional
   B) Associative
   C) Deconstruction
   D) Post-structural
   E) Structural

The correct answer is C:) Deconstruction. To deconstruct an idea, you approach it imagining yourself as someone else. For example, you would approach the idea trying to imagine how a feminist, a conservative, or an anarchist would see the idea. From there, build the ideas up.

16) _____ is the action of writing with no inhibition.

   A) Journaling
   B) Free writing
   C) Brainstorming
   D) Questioning
   E) Hypothesizing

The correct answer is B:) Free writing. Free writing occurs when you sit down and write with no inhibitions. When you free write, you should not be worrying about spelling, grammar, or the ideas that are coming out. Just write!

17) When questioning, make sure you are using _____ questions to field more ideas.

   A) Scientific
   B) Closed
   C) Open
   D) Infinite
   E) Mathematical

The correct answer is C:) Open. Open questions are questions that field varied answers as opposed to closed questions, which field yes/no responses. To make sure ideas develop, use open questions.

18) _____ should only be undertaken when you have a series of facts and would like to argue how they are tied together.

  A) Testing
  B) Analysis
  C) Brainstorming
  D) Free writing
  E) Hypothesizing

The correct answer is E:) Hypothesizing. A hypothesis is an educated guess on how facts are related to each other. If you do not have the facts, you cannot hypothesize.

19) Hypothesizing is dangerous without previous knowledge of a subject because it can _____ your judgment and form biases.

  A) Strengthen
  B) Cloud
  C) Alter
  D) Block
  E) Arrest

The correct answer is B:) Cloud. Not knowing enough of a subject or being unable to formulate an effective argument should prevent you from hypothesizing early. In other words, hypothesizing needs to be carefully done.

20) _____ is one of the most important aspects of becoming a great writer.

  A) Writing perfectly
  B) Publishing
  C) Listening to music
  D) Reading
  E) Attending writing workshops

The correct answer is D:) Reading. A couple of the above answers will help you become a great writer, but besides writing daily, the best thing you can do is to read.

21) The first type of reading is to read _____.

   A) As many different genres as possible
   B) Only the genres that will help with your career
   C) Only self-help books
   D) Nothing
   E) Newspaper articles

The correct answer is A:) As many different genres as possible. Of the two types of reading, the first type is the type of reading you should be doing at all times except when you are focusing on research.

22) When beginning research, your reading should be more _____ than the first type of writing.

   A) Restricted
   B) Varied
   C) Focused
   D) Non-existent
   E) Hyperactive

The correct answer is C:) Focused. When you have your questions figured out and begin to research, your reading should be as focused on that topic as possible. This can be done by making a bibliography and making sure the reading is done for the express purpose of strengthening your writing.

23) Before you begin your focused reading or research, you should develop a _____ that is constructed of books, journal articles, and other readings.

   A) Summer reading list
   B) Historiography
   C) State of the science
   D) Bibliography
   E) Blurb

The correct answer is D:) Bibliography. A bibliography is a list of works used for research. You can find bibliographies for a wide array of subjects online and at the end of books, or you can ask a librarian to help you develop one.

24) Once you begin your reading, you should begin with the _____ types of books.

   A) Utterly specific
   B) Broad overview
   C) Scholarly
   D) Narrative
   E) Critically acclaimed

The correct answer is B:) Broad overview. It is a good idea to start your reading with a book that offers an overview of the subject you are researching. This gives you the "larger picture" that can help you contextualize the other information you will learn.

25) A published bibliography—whether online or in print—will include _____, which are groupings of thought that can help you keep the literature organized.

   A) Genres
   B) Thoughts
   C) Outlines
   D) Schools
   E) Colleges

The correct answer is D:) Schools. Many subjects have quite a large number of books dedicated to it. As such, bibliographies and scholarship will often divide the literature into "schools" of thought that often have opposing views on the same subject.

26) The best way to take notes with your reading is from _____ to _____.

   A) Broadest, most focused
   B) Most focused, broadest
   C) Rarest, easiest found
   D) Easiest found, rarest
   E) Older, newer

The correct answer is A:) Broadest to most focused. You should start your focused reading with the broader reads, understanding the larger picture that will allow you to fit the more focused reads into context.

27) The best thing you can do prior to beginning your writing is to create an _____.

   A) Office assistant
   B) Ghost writer
   C) Outline
   D) Bibliography
   E) Index

The correct answer is C:) Outline. Outlines can vary in complexity, from very simple—including only your main points and how they fit together—to extremely complex, which includes a plan for almost every sentence.

28) If outlines do not work for you, you can also create a _____ which allows you to visually see the information that will be included in the writing piece.

   A) Outline
   B) Mind map
   C) Visual palace
   D) Homonym
   E) Doodle

The correct answer is B:) Mind map. A mind map is particularly useful for fiction writers, allowing them to see how each smaller story that will be used fits together into the grand narrative.

29) When creating a mind map, you start first with the _____.

   A) Outline
   B) Evidence
   C) Conclusion
   D) Primary question
   E) Subsequent question

The correct answer is D:) Primary question. Here, the primary question refers to the major question you arrived at earlier that is driving your research.

30) For narrative pieces, you should put the main parts of the narrative in the _____ of the mind map.

   A) Center
   B) Corners
   C) Left-center
   D) Right-center
   E) Middle-top

The correct answer is B:) Corners. If you are creating a mind map for the narrative type of writing, you put the main idea at the center of the paper and put setting, character, plot, and timeline in the corners. Rather than doing this for the whole book in one map, do one for each scene you are planning to do.

31) By the time you actually start writing the piece, _____ of the work should already be done.

   A) None
   B) Some
   C) A little
   D) All
   E) Most

The correct answer is E:) Most. This shows how important the preparation is in writing. By the time you get to the drafting stage, much of the information, construction, and framework of the paper should be completed through your research, notes, and outlines. However, not all of the work is done, just a good chunk.

32) When organizing a nonfiction piece of writing, your _____ should be clearly written at the beginning.

   A) Evidence
   B) Primary assertion
   C) Sub-evidence
   D) Denouement
   E) Climax

The correct answer is B:) Primary assertion. Your primary assertion, main point, argument, or conclusion—whatever you want to call it—needs to clearly articulated right at the beginning before anything else is introduced.

33) Organizing a fiction piece is a bit freer because you only have to pay attention to the _____ of the writing.

   A) Evidence
   B) Primary assertion
   C) Flow
   D) Conclusion
   E) Cast

The correct answer is C:) Flow. While the making of a good fiction piece involves ensuring that the characters, climax, plot, and setting are in place and well-articulated, for our purposes here in writing the piece well, it has to flow.

34) Each piece of nonfiction writing must have an introduction, a _____, and a conclusion.

   A) Body
   B) Sub-introduction
   C) Pre-conclusion
   D) Chapter
   E) Denouement

The correct answer is A:) Body. Each piece of nonfiction writing has to have an introduction, a body, and a conclusion. For argumentative essays, each section has its own purpose, and the body is the only section of these three that can have multiple parts.

35) The _____ introduces a general idea in language that isn't too specific but is still straightforward in language.

   A) Concluding sentence
   B) Second sentence
   C) Third sentence
   D) Topic sentence
   E) Fifth sentence

The correct answer is D:) Topic sentence. The introduction to a paragraph, the topic sentence lays out what is going to be communicated in that paragraph. It should be a summation of that information, and should not go in too deep in terms of depth.

36) Each paragraph should have good _____ to make sure the information flows between paragraphs.

    A) Transitions
    B) Formulations
    C) Conclusions
    D) Introductions
    E) Encapsulations

The correct answer is A:) Transitions. Generally included in the topic sentence of paragraphs, transitional words and phrases ensure that the information from one paragraph is connected and carries over into the next.

37) The _____ phase of writing is the single most important aspect of writing.

    A) Drafting
    B) Pre-writing
    C) Editing
    D) Publication
    E) Indexing

The correct answer is C:) Editing. The final phase of the writing process, editing/proofreading, is the most important section of the writing process. It is in this phase that terrible writing can be turned into the next great novel, with proper attention and a close eye to style.

38) You should edit your paper _____ in order to make it as strong as possible.

    A) Only once
    B) Twice
    C) As many times as you can
    D) A couple of times
    E) Zero times

The correct answer is C:) As many times as you can. The more you edit, the better the writing will be. Moreover, each time you should be paying attention to something new, be it style, grammar, or spelling.

39) One way to make sure that you don't miss any misspelled words is to _____.

   A) Read it backwards
   B) Run it through a spell check
   C) Check each and every word in a dictionary
   D) Don't worry about it; someone else will
   E) Read it through at least twice

The correct answer is A:) Read it backwards. While some of the other answers are possible (except D of course!) reading the piece in reverse order forces you to pay attention to the spelling of words.

40) Once you have proofread the paper for mistakes, you should read through the piece a few more times taking a _____ stance.

   A) Frustrated
   B) Forced
   C) Deconstructionist
   D) Post-structural
   E) Philosophical

The correct answer is C:) Deconstructionist. As was detailed throughout the chapter, reading through a piece taking a deconstructionist stance forces you to see the paper through the eyes of a reader. Doing so can bring out holes in the paper, argument, or story that can help.

41) In the world of nonfiction writing, the _____ is king.

   A) Letter
   B) Evidence
   C) Tables
   D) Conclusion
   E) Argument

The correct answer is E:) Argument. Any nonfiction that you read, save for popular informative reads, will have an argument that drives the writing forward.

42) The primary component of an argument is the _____.

    A) Assertion
    B) Evidence
    C) Index
    D) Bibliography
    E) Citations

The correct answer is A:) Assertion. Throughout the chapter we utilized the term "assertion" to depict the primary stance that is supported throughout an argument. However, the term can be called numerous things including conclusion or argument.

43) Logicians divide the study of an argument into _____ categories.

    A) One
    B) Four
    C) Ten
    D) Two
    E) Thirteen

The correct answer is D:) Two. Logicians will divide arguments based on the degree to which a conclusion, assertion, or argument can be "proven."

44) _____ is the type of argument that can be completely proven.

    A) Deductive argument
    B) Inductive argument
    C) Scientific argument
    D) Mathematical argument
    E) Historical argument

The correct answer is A:) Deductive argument. Called "top-down logic," it involves a series of premises, each of which can be accepted as true, linked together to prove another premise.

45) The second argumentative category is _____ logic, which can only strongly suggest the veracity of an assertion.

   A) Deductive
   B) Inductive
   C) Scientific
   D) Mathematical
   E) Historical

The correct answer is B:) Inductive. Inductive logic involves the chaining together of evidence to supply a strong level of support of an assertion, but can never be proved to 100% conclusiveness.

46) The argument must be _____, usually in the introduction, to make sure the reader understands it and it is strong.

   A) Clearly stated
   B) Unstated
   C) Absent
   D) Hidden
   E) Split

The correct answer is A:) Clearly stated. If the assertion is not clearly articulated, or remains ambiguous at any point, it will fall apart under scrutiny.

47) The central assertion should have strong, _____ language.

   A) Ambiguous
   B) Passive
   C) Derisive
   D) Active
   E) Gentle

The correct answer is D:) Active. Remember, an active sentence has the subject acting on the direct object. For a simple remembering device, just recall that the phrase "the man kicks the dog" is an active sentence, while the phrase "the dog has been kicked by the man" is passive.

48) The assertion needs to ensure that it takes a _____ on an issue.

   A) Detour
   B) Stance
   C) Summary
   D) Force
   E) Silent

The correct answer is B:) Stance. Simply stating others' arguments is not writing your own argument. You must develop and clearly state your stance on an issue, which is an argument.

49) An extension of the argument is the _____, which states the argument and how the author is going to prove it.

   A) Argument
   B) Evidence
   C) Climax
   D) Thesis
   E) Disclaimer

The correct answer is D:) Thesis. The thesis statement, as stated in the question, lays out the argument and then tells, in a bit of a roundabout way, how that assertion is going to be proven.

50) The thesis statement helps maintain _____ throughout the writing.

   A) Support
   B) Focus
   C) Sway
   D) Explosiveness
   E) Veracity

The correct answer is B:) Focus. This is particularly true in regard to pieces that are longer in length. When the pages add up, maintaining focus is ever important: the more evidence you have, the more you will want to include this statement to make sure the focus is maintained.

51) _____ is any piece of information that can be used to support the main assertion.

   A) Data
   B) Tables
   C) Paragraphs
   D) Sentences
   E) Evidence

The correct answer is E:) Evidence. Evidence can be written words, numbers, data, visual, or sound samples.

52) The _____ is the philosophical litmus test for evidence.

   A) Burden of proof
   B) Numerical amount
   C) Statistical proof
   D) Backing of experts
   E) Popularity

The correct answer is A:) Burden of proof. The burden of proof entails an obligation of the individual arguing to give enough supporting evidence of a claim.

53) The type of evidence you choose to utilize in an argument is based heavily on the _____.

   A) Type of argument
   B) Burden of proof
   C) Mathematical certainty
   D) Audience
   E) Writer

The correct answer is D:) Audience. Some types of evidence are more relevant to some types of audiences, while others work better for another audience. Pay attention to what types of evidence other sources are using and let that help guide you in your choice.

54) Within the burden of proof, evidence can provide _____, which sufficiently proves the claim beyond reasonable doubt.

   A) Direct proof
   B) Circumstantial proof
   C) Circumstantial evidence
   D) Statistical proof
   E) Philosophical proof

The correct answer is A:) Direct proof. Direct proof sufficiently proves the assertion beyond reasonable doubt. As was written in the chapter, this type of evidence is of the "caught red-handed" type of evidence, where arguing against it can be an uphill battle.

55) Evidence that is _____ can only prove an assertion to a certain degree, but multiple pieces of evidence of this type placed together can raise the chances that the assertion is proven.

   A) Direct proof
   B) Circumstantial
   C) Statistical
   D) Philosophical
   E) Rational

The correct answer is B:) Circumstantial. Circumstantial evidence, when put together, can sufficiently prove the veracity of an argument.

56) The _____ is the best way to construct a strong argument from your stance and evidence.

   A) Diocesan Method
   B) Socratic Method
   C) Aristotelian Method
   D) Toulmin Method
   E) Formulaic Method

The correct answer is D) Toulmin Method. The Toulmin Method was developed by a British philosopher and involves the rational construction of an argument using the assertion, evidence, and other bits of information.

57) In the Toulmin Method, the _____ is analysis of the evidence that ties it to the main claim and to other pieces of evidence.

   A) Evidence
   B) Bridge
   C) Backing
   D) Support
   E) Conclusion

The correct answer is B:) Bridge. The bridge should be included throughout the piece and provides a place to analyze and draw out any unstated assumption that affects the argument.

58) The _____ is the section of the Toulmin Method that allows for an explanation of any outside reasoning needed to understand the overall argument.

   A) Argument
   B) Bridge
   C) Backing
   D) Support
   E) Conclusion

The correct answer is C:) Backing. The backing, or "foundation," is a section of the writing that allows you to write in any outside reasoning needed to understand the argument. This can be especially useful if, at first, the evidence doesn't appear to belong.

59) The _____ is the presentation of an opposing claim that is then argued against in the writing through a rebuttal.

   A) Assertion
   B) Backing
   C) Counterclaim
   D) Rebuttal
   E) Conclusion

The correct answer is C:) Counterclaim. The counterclaim can either be a statement summarizing the opposing argument, or can be an entire section. Many writers will include the claims of opposition in the introduction to show how their argument fits into the literature and how they are arguing against others' arguments.

60) Many writers will begin their paper, in the introduction, with an _____ that shows the argument in practice.

    A) Summary
    B) Anecdote
    C) General overview
    D) Introduction sentence
    E) Bullet-points

The correct answer is B:) Anecdote. The anecdote is a short story that sets the pace for the writing, showing how the argument is true by its application in the real world.

61) The introduction should include your _____, which includes both the argument and the evidence you plan on using in the writing.

    A) Conclusion
    B) Argument
    C) Evidence
    D) Index
    E) Thesis statement

The correct answer is E:) Thesis statement. As stated before, the thesis includes both the argument and evidence. In an argumentative essay, you should make sure that the statement is clearly written, in strong, active language, and make sure that it does not give too much away.

62) Many writers include the _____ in the introduction to show how their argument fits into the literature.

    A) Index
    B) Introduction
    C) Counterclaim
    D) Table of contents
    E) Evidence

The correct answer is C:) Counterclaim. The counterclaim is included here to show how the writer's argument will play out in relation to other authors' arguments.

63) The longest section of the piece, due to the amount of information included in it, is the _____.

   A) Introduction
   B) Counterclaim
   C) Argument
   D) Body
   E) Conclusion

The correct answer is D:) Body. The body should carry the brunt of the evidence, analysis, and explanations.

64) The most important aspect of the body is the _____.

   A) Bridge
   B) Evidence
   C) Counterclaim
   D) Conclusion
   E) Introduction

The correct answer is A:) Bridge. While you will be including every piece of evidence you have gathered, the explanation that ties that evidence to the argument is the most important aspect.

65) The _____ should be brought back in at the conclusion to more fully draw out the argument.

   A) Argument
   B) Counterclaim
   C) Evidence
   D) Conclusion
   E) Rebuttal

The correct answer is B:) Counterclaim. By restating the counterclaim, you can bring the paper back into focus at the end.

66) The best thing you can do to be able to identify arguments more readily in reading is to _____.

   A) Ask others
   B) Read the SparkNotes
   C) Read a summary of the book
   D) Read as much as possible
   E) Hope you get lucky

The correct answer is D:) Read as much as possible. The more argument constructions you are exposed to, the more used to finding arguments you will get.

67) The first thing to do when identifying an argument is to _____.

   A) Take a quick read through major sections of the book
   B) Hunt for keywords in the introduction
   C) Assume the argument from the chapter titles
   D) Guess from the title of the book
   E) Guess from the pictures

The correct answer is A:) Take a quick read through major sections of the book. While keywords can be found that indicate an argument or thesis statement, many books do not include such keywords so that the work reads better. Thus, having a tactic that allows you to understand the argument without resorting to a keyword search is the best tactic, and should be the first thing you do.

68) The first sign of a strong argument is _____.

   A) Multiple pages of citations
   B) Numerous pages of evidence
   C) A clearly written and articulated central argument
   D) Multiple pages
   E) A catchy title

The correct answer is C:) A clearly written and articulated central argument. When the assertion is strong, the overall argument will be strong.

69) A strong argument will identify core _____ that drive the rationale behind the stance.

   A) Assumptions
   B) Philosophies
   C) Schools of thought
   D) Formulations
   E) Rationales

The correct answer is A:) Assumptions. Assumptions are unstated thoughts that lie behind the writing. Make sure that when writing you identify these to make sure there are no biases controlling the argument.

70) The most commonly used secondary sources are _____ and _____.

   A) Magazines and newspapers
   B) Newspapers and journal articles
   C) Journal articles and magazine articles
   D) Scholarly books and journal articles
   E) Scholarly books and newspapers.

The correct answer is D:) Scholarly books and journal articles. These provide the most accurate information available to scholars on a given subject.

71) A great location to find books useful to your study are _____ in peer-reviewed journals.

   A) Pictures
   B) Book reviews
   C) Internet URLs
   D) Indexes
   E) Tables of content

The correct answer is B:) Book reviews. Many journals will also include a section on "Books Recently Received" that can provide titles that may be useful to your research.

72) The best way to judge the strength of a source is by reading _____.

   A) The book
   B) The blurb
   C) The table of contents
   D) A book review in a peer-edited journal
   E) A newspaper opinion article

The correct answer is D:) A book review in a peer-edited journal. Here, you will find experts in the field weighing in on the strengths of the source in question, helping you formulate an opinion of the sources.

73) The first tactic in utilizing the information from sources is to _____.

   A) Re-write the entire source verbatim
   B) Imply that you read the source
   C) Summarize
   D) Quote from the text
   E) Completely forget about it and move on

The correct answer is: C:) Summarize. Summarizing is a brief overview of the text, providing the argument and any "between the line" assumptions that can help your argument.

74) Another tactic for using a source is the _____, which is a shorter summation of the source.

   A) Paraphrase
   B) Summary
   C) Quote
   D) Denouement
   E) Climax

The correct answer is A:) Paraphrase. To paraphrase a text, you only write the argument and make sure that it is only a sentence long, at most.

75) One way to quote a text is to use _____ quotations, which places the quote in your writing and allows for analysis prior to, during, and after the quotation.

   A) Block
   B) In-text
   C) Conclusive
   D) Inconclusive
   E) Argumentative

The correct answer is B:) In-text. In-text quotations should be shorter and should only be used to supplement a thought in your analysis.

76) Another way to quote a source is to use the _____ quote, which is a longer quotation to give more information from the source.

   A) Block
   B) In-text
   C) Conclusive
   D) Inconclusive
   E) Argumentative

The correct answer is A:) Block. The block quote can be multiple lines, but should not be any more than five lines. For particularly longer quotes, you can utilize the ellipses to cut out unneeded words.

77) The _____ style of citation is used primarily in the liberal arts or humanities.

   A) Chicago
   B) APA
   C) MLA
   D) Harvard
   E) Washington

The correct answer is C:) MLA. Standing for "Modern Languages Association," MLA citation utilizes parenthetical in-text citations that include the author, date of publication, and page number.

78) The _____ is used in a wide-variety of books due to its ability to cite but not break up the writing with unneeded parentheses.

    A) Chicago
    B) APA
    C) MLA
    D) Harvard
    E) Washington

The correct answer is A:) Chicago. Chicago citation utilizes footnotes and endnotes, which provide a citation style that helps keep the focus on the writing, rather than breaking it up with parentheses.

79) The _____ style citation is similar to MLA, but is used more often in the social sciences.

    A) Chicago
    B) APA
    C) MLA
    D) Harvard
    E) Washington

The correct answer is B:) APA. Standing for "American Psychological Association," the APA uses in-text parenthetical citations while using a slightly different bibliographic page that does not include source authors' first names (only initials), quotations on titles, or italics.

80) Rottenberg's method is based on which of the following individuals

    A) Roger
    B) Truman
    C) Toulmin
    D) Truman

The correct answer is C:) Toulmin. Annette Rottenberg's theory is closely based on Stephen Toulmin's theory.

81) The concept or study that observes how results can be reached through logical reasoning, such as healthy debate and conversation, is called _____.

   A) Augmentation theory
   B) Argumentation theory
   C) Extortion theory
   D) Observation theory

The correct answer is B:) Argumentation theory. The other answers are fictional options. Argumentation theory specifically studies the threads between how conclusions are reached using rules and logic and can be found in areas such as the law.

82) The _____, named after an English philosopher, breaks down the elements used to make a persuasive argument. It includes the elements of claim, grounds, warrant, backing, qualifier, and rebuttal.

   A) Rogerian argument theory
   B) Rottenberg's argument theory
   C) Truman's argument theory
   D) Toulmin's argument theory

The correct answer is D:) Toulmin's argument theory. English philosopher, Stephen Toulmin, sought to break arguments down into basic parts to show how one can state and support their argument by ensuring all parts are provided.

83) The link between the actual grounds for an argument or specific data that legitimizes the claim is called a _____.

   A) Warrant
   B) Backing
   C) Qualifier
   D) Rebuttal

The correct answer is A:) Warrant. The other answers are all part of a persuasive argument as outlined via Toulmin's argument theory.

84) The _____ warrant relies on the audience's ability to lend credence to the source providing the evidence during a persuasive argument. It is also called the ethos-based appeal.

   A) Substantive
   B) Explicit
   C) Authoritative
   D) Implicit

The correct answer is C:) Authoritative. The other answers are all other forms of a warrant. The authoritative warrant specifically seeks to provide credibility to an evidence set simply due to the source of where the evidence came from or the source that presented the evidence.

85) The warrant method that relies on a direct and factual link between similar evidence bases and arguments to the point that because one is true the other must be as well is called _____.

   A) Substantive
   B) Motivational
   C) Authoritative
   D) Implicit

The correct answer is A:) Substantive. The other answers are all other forms of a warrant. The substantive warrant is sometimes called a warrant by analogy or warrant by cause because it relies on the factual connection between similar cases to justify the validity of the argument (i.e. one set of evidence has been proven to be valid so this similar set must also be valid too).

86) The _____ warrant plays on the emotions and values of the directed audience as the grounds for why evidence should be accept as valid in an argument.

   A) Substantive
   B) Motivational
   C) Authoritative
   D) Implicit

The correct answer is B:) Motivational. The other answers are all other forms of a warrant. The motivational warrant uses the values and beliefs of the intended audience with the intent of receiving evidence credibility because of those held beliefs.

87) The warrant method that relies on the intended audience to make the logical connections between the evidence and the claim is called _____.

   A) Substantive
   B) Explicit
   C) Authoritative
   D) Implicit

The correct answer is D:) Implicit. During a persuasive argument, the person making the claim can use implicit warrants instead of making a direct connection with an evidence set because they are relying on the audience to connect the dots.

88) The warrant method that relies on making a direct evidence connection with a claim for the intended audience is called _____.

   A) Substantive
   B) Authoritative
   C) Explicit
   D) Implicit

The correct answer is C:) Explicit. The other answers are all other forms of a warrant. The explicit warrant seeks to provide the direct connections between evidence and a claim to make certain that the intended audience understands the connection and the validity of the claim from the evidence provided.

89) When making a claim, a significant part of preparing your argument should be to _____ to understand best how the audience might interpret the claim and evidence provided due to their held beliefs or life experiences.

   A) Examine the warrant
   B) Examine the audience
   C) Examine the assumptions
   D) Examine the claim

The correct answer is C:) Examine the assumptions. The other answers are all variations on the correct answer.

90) The _____ is an argumentative theory technique that seeks to resolve conflict by finding the common ground within a particular argument or debate.

   A) Rottenberg's argument
   B) Rogerian argument
   C) Truman's argument
   D) Toulmin's argument

The correct answer is B:) Rogerian argument. The Rogerian argument is used during a persuasive argument to convey to the audience that the presenter understands their viewpoint and validates their common held beliefs and that in turn creates a connection between the parties to help the argument gain validity.

91) While a warrant is considered a more general, broad connection that can apply to numerous arguments, a _____ is a more specific connection based upon time and place.

   A) Claim
   B) Observation
   C) Backing
   D) Assumption

The correct answer is A:) Claim. The other answers are all other parts of a persuasive argument or fictional answers.

92) The act of _____ is when you take a source of information and translate it into one's own words.

   A) Attributing
   B) Quoting
   C) Paraphrasing
   D) Backing

The correct answer is C:) Paraphrasing. When paraphrasing, the writer/speaker seeks to convey words/sources that are not their own, but that they attribute to the original source. Often, paraphrasing shortens the original writing to suit the user's needs.

93) The act of _____ is when the main points of source material are put into one's own words and is significantly shorter than the source material.

   A) Quoting
   B) Attributing
   C) Backing
   D) Summarizing

The correct answer is D:) Summarizing. While similar to paraphrasing, summarizing is significantly shorter than paraphrasing and only focuses on the main points of an original source.

94) The act of _____ is when source data is used word for word within an argument or document.

   A) Attributing
   B) Quoting
   C) Paraphrasing
   D) Backing

The correct answer is B:) Quoting. When quoting a source, the words used must be in quotation marks and word for word from the original. It must also be directly attributed to the original author or document.

95) The thesis statement is usually one to two sentences long and can be found in the _____ sentence in the introductory paragraph.

   A) First
   B) Last
   C) Second
   D) Third

The correct answer is B:) Last. The point of making the thesis statement the last sentence of the introductory paragraph is to convey your message and leave the reader with that as their last impression.

#  Test-Taking Strategies

Here are some test-taking strategies that are specific to this test and to other DSST tests in general:

- Keep your eyes on the time. Pay attention to how much time you have left.
- Read the entire question and read all the answers. Many questions are not as hard to answer as they may seem. Sometimes, a difficult sounding question really only is asking you how to read an accompanying chart. Chart and graph questions are on most DANTES/DSST tests and should be an easy free point.
- If you don't know the answer immediately, the new computer-based testing lets you mark questions and come back to them later if you have time.
- Read the wording carefully. Some words can give you hints to the right answer. There are no exceptions to an answer when there are words in the question such as always, all or none. If one of the answer choices includes most or some of the right answers, but not all, then that is not the answer. Here is an example:

    The primary colors include all of the following:
    A) Red, Yellow, Blue, Green
    B) Red, Green, Yellow
    C) Red, Orange, Yellow
    D) Red, Yellow, Blue

    Although item A includes all the right answers, it also includes an incorrect answer, making it incorrect. If you didn't read it carefully, was in a hurry, or didn't know the material well, you might fall for this.

- Make a guess on a question that you do not know the answer to. There is no penalty for an incorrect answer. Eliminate the answer choices that you know are incorrect. For example, this will let your guess be a 1 in 3 chance instead.

# Test Preparation

How much you need to study depends on your knowledge of a subject area. If you are interested in literature, took it in school, or enjoy reading then your study and preparation for the literature or humanities test will not need to be as intensive as that of someone who is new to literature.

This book is much different than the regular DANTES study guides. This book actually teaches you the information that you need to know to pass the test. If you are particularly interested in an area, or feel that you want more information, do a quick search online. We've tried not to include too much depth in areas that are not as essential on the test. Everything in this book will be on the test. It is important to understand all major theories and concepts listed in the table of contents. It is also important to know any bolded words.

Don't worry if you do not understand or know a lot about the area. With minimal study, you can complete and pass the test.

#  Legal Note

All rights reserved. This Study Guide, Book and Flashcards are protected under the US Copyright Law. No part of this book or study guide or flashcards may be reproduced, distributed or stored in a retrieval system, or transmitted in any form or by any means, electronic, mechanical, photocopying, recording, or otherwise, without the prior written permission of the publisher Breely Crush Publishing LLC.

# FLASHCARDS

This section contains flashcards for you to use to further your understanding of the material and test yourself on important concepts, names or dates. Read the term or question then flip the page over to check the answer on the back. Keep in mind that this information may not be covered in the text of the study guide. Take your time to study the flashcards, you will need to know and understand these concepts to pass the test.

| | |
|---|---|
| **Nominative Case** | **Objective Case** |
| **Possessive Case** | **Compound Personal Pronouns** |
| **Relative Pronouns** | **Interrogative Pronouns** |
| **Indefinite Pronouns** | **Agreement in Subject and Verb** |

| | |
|---|---|
| Me, you, her, him, us, the | I, you, she, he, we, you, they |
| Myself, yourself, himself, herself, itself, ourselves, yourselves, themselves | My, mine, your, yours, his, her, hers, its, our, ours, their, theirs |
| Who, which, what | Who, that, which, what |
| The same in singular or plural form | All, any, both, each, either, everybody, none, one, several, some, someone |

# Diction Errors

# Idiom Errors

# Modifiers

# Verbs

# Base Form of Verbs

# Verb Form with -s

# Past Tense Verb

# Past Participle Verb

| | |
|---|---|
| Expressions that are not always clear from the meaning of the words (kick the bucket) | Incorrect word choices |
| Tell what the subject does or what is done to it | Describe words |
| He/she/it plays | I play |
| I have played | I played |

| | |
|---|---|
| **Present Participle** | **Fragment** |
| **Comma Splice** | **Run-on Sentence** |
| **Topic Sentence** | **Restatement or Restriction** |
| **Illustration** | **Analysis** |

| | |
|---|---|
| An incomplete sentence that is punctuated as if it were complete | I am playing |
| Two independent clauses that are not separated by a conjunction or proper punctuation | Two independent clauses containing a comma |
| The second sentence can restate or restrict what was written in the first sentence, making the subject more specific | The first sentence introducing the subject of a paragraph |
| Explain, interpret, and contextualize the illustrations that have been made | This section of the paragraph consists of the illustrations (evidence, data, facts, quotes, ect.) that support your topic |

| | |
|---|---|
| Conclusion | Accept - define |
| Except - define | Affect (vb.) - define |
| Effect - define | All right - spelled correctly? |
| Alright - spelled correctly? | Among |

| | |
|---|---|
| To receive | The final sentence (or two) might review what the paragraph has discussed, and/or reemphasize what is being suggested |
| To influence, to change | To exclude |
| Correct spelling | To accomplish (vb.); a result (n.) |
| When referring to more than two | Incorrect spelling |

| | |
|---|---|
| **Between** | **Continual** |
| **Continous** | **Disinterested** |
| **Uninterested** | **Emigrate** |
| **Immigrate** | **Eminent** |

| | |
|---|---|
| Recurring actions, repeated regularly and frequently | When referring to only two |
| Impartial | Occurring without interruption |
| One emigrates from a place | Not interested |
| Outstanding, distinguished | One immigrates to a place |

| | |
|---|---|
| **Imminent** | **Ensure** |
| **Insure** | **Father** |
| **Further** | **Fewer** |
| **Less** | **Good** |

| To guarantee; to make safe | Threatening to happen soon |
|---|---|
| Describes distance | To provide insurance against loss |
| Used when nouns can be counted and made plural (fewer students) | Additionally; suggests quantity or degree |
| An adjective before a noun or after a linking verb (look good) | Used when nouns can't be counted or made plural (less homework) |

| | |
|---|---|
| **Well** | **Respectfully** |
| **Respectively** | **Set** |
| **Sit** | **Unquestionable** |
| **Unquestioned** | **No exceptions** |

| | |
|---|---|
| Courteously | An adverb when referring to how an action is performed |
| To put or to place | Each in the order given |
| Indisputable | To be seated |
| Always, every, all, only, never, none, not, must, necessary | Has not been questioned |

# NOTES

# NOTES

NOTES

## NOTES

NOTES

## NOTES

# NOTES

# NOTES

# NOTES

## NOTES

NOTES

## NOTES

NOTES

# NOTES

# NOTES

# NOTES

# NOTES

## NOTES

# NOTES

# NOTES

# NOTES

## NOTES

# NOTES

# NOTES

# NOTES

# NOTES

# NOTES

## NOTES

# NOTES

# NOTES

# NOTES

# NOTES

# NOTES

# NOTES

# NOTES

# NOTES

# NOTES

## NOTES

# NOTES

# NOTES

www.ingramcontent.com/pod-product-compliance
Lightning Source LLC
Chambersburg PA
CBHW081833300426
44116CB00014B/2575